The Castle Green at Hereford

—

A Landscape of Ritual, Royalty and Recreation

The Castle Green at Hereford

–

A Landscape of Ritual, Royalty and Recreation

by

David Whitehead

Logaston Press

LOGASTON PRESS
Little Logaston, Logaston,
Woonton, Almeley, Herefordshire HR3 6QH
logastonpress.co.uk

First published by Logaston Press 2007
Copyright © David Whitehead 2007

ISBN
978 1904396 77 2

Set in Times New Roman by Logaston Press
and printed in Great Britain by
Cromwell Press Ltd., Trowbridge

Cover Illustration – Derek Foxton photograph

Contents

This book is dedicated to

Philip Styles (1905-1976)

who stimulated my interest in
the history of the West Midlands

List of Plates

Sources of Illustrations

by kind permission of:

Dr. Derek Foxton
Figs. 47, 85, 86, 93; Plates 1, 9

Bruce Coplestone-Crow
Fig. 4

Ron Shoesmith
Figs. 8, 9, 10, 15, 18, 19, 96, 97, 99; Plates 8, 10, 11, 13, 14

Archaeological Investigations Ltd. (and Owen Williams for Fig. 34)
Fig. 34; Plate 2

Dr. and Mrs. Heijn
Plate 4 (painting by B. Byron)

Sotheby's
Figs. 66, 67, 69

Warden and Fellows of Merton College, Oxford
Fig. 32 (Merton College Library D.3.30, no. 7)

Trustees of the British Museum
Plate 3

Birmingham Art Gallery and Museum
Fig. 30

Worcester Record Office
Fig. 45

Hereford Record Office
Figs. 43, 60, 63, 77, 80, 81, 83, 84, 87, 91, 98; Plates 16, 17

Hereford City Library
Figs. 16, 44, 46, 50, 51, 52, 53, 55, 56, 57, 58, 59, 68, 70, 72, 73, 88; Plates 5, 6

The remainder belong to the author

Preface and Acknowledgements

Castle Green is the hidden gem of Hereford. To find it, concealed behind the streetscape and beyond the Cathedral, it has to be stalked via narrow streets. For the tourist or the resident recently domiciled in the city, it is an exciting find and, indeed, a mystery, since there is little information about its nature and history. The natives of Hereford take it for granted. It provides a useful shortcut from the city centre to the suburbs; it is a convenient place to walk the dog or take quiet recreation and, more recently, to attend a 'fayre'– bands, food and conviviality. For the young people of the city it is a refuge from the more regulated adult world and on a summer evening a place for the gathering of the clans. For young and old the Castle Green is a special place that breathes distinctiveness and discreetly nourishes the spirit. Its past history as a devotional focus, a necropolis and royal palace is all but forgotten and it is the object of this book to demonstrate just how complex the ebb and flow of human activity on this unassuming green space has been in the past.

My own love affair with Castle Green commenced in 1972 when the infant Civic Trust, the city's amenity society, learnt that plans were being drawn up by the then Hereford City Council to stabilise the castle cliff with a concrete promenade and 'grasscrete' – a material used in municipal car parks – laid on the river bank. As the secretary of the Trust it became my duty to organise a campaign to preserve several centuries of character. It did not take much research to discover that from the mid-18th century Castle Green had been deliberately nurtured as a picturesque landscape and was an important incident in an aesthetic movement closely associated with the Wye and in particular with Herefordshire. The Civic Trust's campaign was only partially successful. The 'grasscrete 'went down and members of the Trust scrambled along the cliff planting year-old saplings of native trees in the small openings left in the blanket of concrete. The Trust's vice-chairman, Ray Boddington, watered the young trees every day during a particularly hot summer and today, a forest flourishes on the river bank. This was not quite what we anticipated but it will provide an opportunity for artistic landscaping by the Friends of Castle Green who, like the ingenious sculptor who finds in every block of stone a fine statue, may discover prospects, framed in the rough greenery.

In the midst of the 'improvements' in 1973, Ron Shoesmith carried out an excavation on the southern corner of the Green and found buildings associated with the minster church of St. Guthlac and around it, an extensive burial ground extending back to the 7th century A.D. Following the excavation the present writer was invited to carry out some research to provide an historical framework for the excavation. This was subsequently published in the first of the four volumes of *Hereford City Excavations* by the Council for British Archaeology in 1980. The excavation of St. Guthlac's put Castle Green on the archaeological map of England and during the last 25 years there has been much academic discussion, as well as popular speculation, about the place of the Green in the early history of Hereford and especially, its relationship with the Cathedral. St. Guthlac's is revisited in this volume in the light of recent research both in Herefordshire and in similar sites elsewhere in Britain. The idea that there was also a royal palace on Castle Green, the predecessor of the Norman Castle, is also developed, providing a new line of inquiry, which even if it turns out to be an 'aunt Sally' may stimulate further serious research.

Thirty years teaching Medieval History at Hereford Sixth Form College, including a special paper on Edward the Confessor and the Norman Conquest, made me suspicious of the accepted story of the foundation of the castle at Hereford by Ralph 'the Timid'. So an alternative interpretation of the evolution of the castle is provided here, which again may fall at the first hurdle, but hopefully will open up an interesting debate. The subsequent story of the development of the castle is the least original of part of this study. As my footnotes will show there are excellent accounts of the castle elsewhere. No doubt a more diligent scholar than the present writer, prepared to spend some time working on the public records in London, would be able to add considerable detail to the story and particularly help understand the evolution of individual components of the building.

Equally, the Civil War in Herefordshire is well-charted territory, but to link the two major sections of this study, the detailed story of the last inglorious days of the castle, as a royalist and parliamentary stronghold, needed to be told. I hope that even those who know the subject well will find one or two new insights here.

In 2004 I was asked by Herefordshire Council to provide the historical section for an application to the Heritage Lottery Fund for a grant to restore Castle Green as a polished municipal park. In the event the application was deferred, but the historical research into the park has been developed here. In Castle Green, Hereford has a magnificent open public space with a pedigree extending back to the early 18th century, which is only paralleled in one or two other great cities. Perhaps one of the most touching moments in my research came when I delved into the minute book of the Society of Tempers, who laid out the picturesque park in the mid-18th century, and found that they were enamoured with druidical role play. Intangibly, it appears, they had picked up the ancient vibrations of Castle Green and re-connected themselves with the churchmen who colonised the Green in the 'Celtic twilight' over 1,000 years before. Two hundred years after the demise of the Tempers, I hope this book provides a connected history of a unique corner of the kingdom.

I should like to thank Ron Shoesmith, whose excavations in the early 1970s enhanced my interest in Castle Green and who, rather fittingly, saw this book through the complex process of publication and allowed me to illustrate it with many of his drawings and photographs. Andy Johnson, for asking for the whole story. Keith Ray, who commissioned the history of the park. Joe Hillaby, Jean O' Donnell, John Eisel and Tim Hoverd, for illuminating conversations on the Green. The staff at the Hereford Reference Library, the Record Office and the Cathedral Library, who showed unfailing patience and allowed me to use many of their illustrations. The various people and organisations listed on page viii, who also allowed me to make use of their illustrations and especially Derek Foxton who, as usual, was very generous with his material and provided the cover photograph and finally, the Friends of Castle Green – all power to their elbows!

David Whitehead, Hafod Road, Hereford.
April, 2007

CHAPTER I

Introduction

Making a Landscape

It is difficult to imagine Herefordshire just after the last Ice Age, say 15,000 B.C., when the 'Whole county was largely a lake irregularly broken by islands, some ancient hills, other moraine heaps. [Through this] the river Wye wound its way leisurely, removing the clay, shifting the sand and smoothing the pebbles'.[1] At one point in this era the main route of the Wye appears to have been below Aylestone Hill, coming from Stretton Sugwas, across Widemarsh, cutting into Eign Hill and washing up against the slopes of Dinedor Hill.[2] The sites of the Cathedral and Castle Green were at this

Fig. 1. The gravel deposits on Castle Cliffe being stabilised in 1973.

date connected by land to Putson and Blackmarston but a little later, a sudden surge of water, produced as the Little Welsh Glacier continued to disintegrate, cut a new course for the Wye through the high ground at Belmont and Breinton; pushing aside the existing gravel banks around the site of the city, it smashed into a prominent ridge of gravel, creating the site on which Hereford Castle and Cathedral were eventually built. Without the concrete defences laid on the bank in the 1970s, the river would still be 'removing the clay, shifting the sand and smoothing the pebbles' (Fig. 1).

Castle Green (and the city) emerged from this turmoil as a dry ridge surrounded to the north and east by a wet corridor, aptly called 'the wide-marsh'. Here in 1966 deep trenches cut through three feet of sedge peat, which, when dried, was burnt by the workmen on their brazier.[3] The water that remained in this area percolated under the city and in earlier times could be reached with wells 16 or 18 feet deep and where the gravels gave way to the river, there were springs such as the Pipe Well in Gwynne Street and St. Ethelbert's Well beneath Castle Green.

As the temperature began to rise the Wye lost much of its energy and the gravel island gradually dried out.[4] Grasses, followed by birch and willow, began to colonise the raised ground and, much later, around 8,000 B.C., hazels, limes and oaks arrived (Fig. 2).[5] The base and roots of a large oak tree were found 12 to 14 feet below the surface, behind the Methodist chapel in Bridge Street[6]. However, the goats, boar and red deer, whose bones have been found in and around the city, presumably kept the vegetation low and, as a result, Castle Green would have looked like open parkland or, perhaps, like 'broomy hill'. Significantly, one version of the *Life of St. Ethelbert* refers to the burial place of the saint as *fernlega* – 'the ferny-place'. This may, of course, be a monkish invention, but it certainly suits the immediate environment of Hereford in this remote period and has parallels with Shrewsbury –*scrobbsberi* – the 'shrubby place or burh'. In Welsh both places are simply referred to as the 'place of trees'.[7]

Fig. 2. Small-leaved Lime (Tilia cordata) – *a post-glacial tree still to be found on the wild slopes of Castle Green (2006).*

Fig. 3. The 'by-ford' below Castle Green (2006).

A Place Set Aside

The arrival of Neolithic people in *c*.4,000 B.C. with their grazing animals and increasing demand for timber would, no doubt, have reduced the tree-cover on the gravels even further. Indeed, the jawbone of a goat, found at Stonebow in 1866, is just as likely to be a sheep, as in skeletal terms the two are difficult to distinguish.[8] Notwithstanding much excavation and observation on Castle Green, not one flint scraper has been recovered to suggest the presence of early man. Neolithic and Bronze Age flints and a few axes have been found all round the city but apart from a small assemblage of scrapers and arrow heads, found in Victoria Street in 1968, and a collection of 35 flints from Nash's Sack Warehouse site, on the southern bank of the Wye in 1985, there is little firm evidence for prehistoric occupation within the city.[9] The latter, found close to the site of Hereford's river crossing, suggests, perhaps that the ford was in use. During the subsequent Iron Age, with the Hereford basin ringed with hill-forts, it is difficult to imagine that such a convenient crossing place on the river was ignored. Indeed, it is likely that the second ford beneath Castle Green came into existence at an early date as a by-ford (Fig. 3). If any herdsman cast his eyes upwards towards the green plateau, he might well have admired the grazing cattle – the bones of which dominate the archaeological record for this period around Hereford. In the late Iron Age, 41% of the bones found at the hill-fort of Sutton Walls, north-east of the city, came from cattle. This figure is very close to the 40% of similar bones from several sites in Hereford itself during the Saxon and medieval periods.[10]

Most modern authorities believe the Romans utilised the ford beneath the Bishop's Palace for a major military route running from Chester to Caerleon. This appears to have been diverted with the foundation of a civilian settlement at Kenchester (*Magnis*), which was served by a bridge crossing the Wye at Old Weir. Although the original road was aligned with the ford, so far it has not been located in the city. However, a brief glimpse of Roman floor material outside the

Library in Broad Street and close to its suggested route, suggests that there may be Roman building beside the road. Further Roman finds were exposed on the same alignment during the excavation in advance of the new library building at Hereford Cathedral, although the archaeologists found no trace of any substantial Roman building in the vicinity of the west end of the cathedral.[11] However, this cumulative evidence, perhaps, begins to provide some context for the two Roman altars, found with other Roman building material, in Victoria Street in 1968.

Along with another altar found in the 19th century in St. John Street, these are likely to have been recycled from a local source rather than Kenchester, especially as the two in Victoria Street were being reused for a mundane purpose in a corn-drying oven. Perhaps we can be a little more confident that there was a Roman presence at the heart of Hereford but it must have been on a small scale and possibly, transitory. No Roman material has come from Castle Green – it remained a place set aside from the community.[12]

CHAPTER II

Ritual : The Minster Church

The Lost Centuries

As an initial step, a firm understanding of the early topography of Hereford is necessary. The cathedral precinct and the streets that approach it – St. John Street, Church Street and Broad Street – occupy the most convenient platform on the Hereford terrace (Fig. 19). Broad Street originally led down – through the Bishop's Palace garden – to the ford, whilst to its west there was a marshy area which was later called the 'king's ditch'. Two named springs fed this peaty morass – *rotholveswalle* –'cattle well' (Aubrey Street) and *pipewele* – 'spring with a conduit' (Gwynne Street).[13] Later in the Saxon era this area was bridged, but in the post-Roman period it would have been an impediment for settlement to the west of Broad Street. Across the present cathedral close there was another wet area, less extensive than the 'king's ditch', but marked by St. Ethelbert's well, which in early documents is always referred to as a *fons* or fountain and in 1250 as '*fontem beati Ethelberti*'.[14] In the early 18th century water from its spring still ran down to the Wye and in the Middle Ages, presumably fed into the moat of the castle. The river end of Quay Street is still much lower than the surrounding land and in earlier times Castle Green would rise up steeply from this little valley, becoming a place quite distinct from the settlement on the main terrace

The early history of Castle Green, where eventually the minster church of St. Guthlac would appear, is tied up intimately with the arrival of the cathedral. The most recent account of this, outlined by John Blair, suggests that the bishop and his church arrived rather late on the Hereford terrace and were 'inserted into an older religious landscape dominated by minsters like Ledbury and Leominster'. He further believes that Hereford may have existed as a rural settlement onto which the cathedral was grafted. There was also a religious community already here, which may have enjoyed the corn, dried in the sophisticated ovens found in Victoria Street in 1968 and acted as custodians of a burial ground on Castle Green. Blair compares Hereford with North Elmham in Norfolk where the arrival of a bishop led to the reorganisation of the village plan to create a regular grid, which ultimately became the present town plan.[15]

It is inevitable that discussions about the origins of Hereford should focus upon ecclesiastical rather than political organisation. For the former there is at least a framework of documentary references, whereas virtually nothing is known about the latter. However, it seems clear that from the 5th to the 8th centuries Hereford was part of a sub-Roman world (British or Celtic, if you like) ruled by minor Christian princes, which stretched westwards into Wales and south-west across the Severn into Somerset and Devon.[16] Later Welsh sources, much corrupted by bardic and antiquarian intervention, regard the

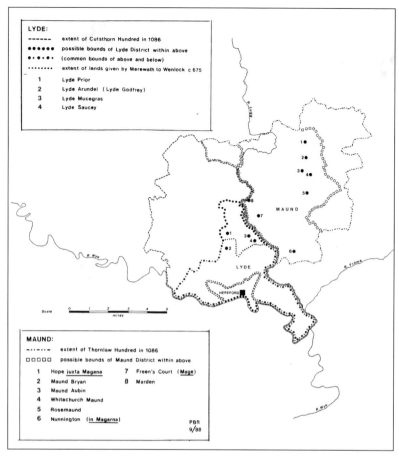

LYDE:
- `------` extent of Cutsthorn Hundred in 1086
- `●●●●●●` possible bounds of Lyde District within above
- `●·●·●·●` (common bounds of above and below)
- `·········` extent of lands given by Merewalh to Wenlock c 675

1 Lyde Prior
2 Lyde Arundel (Lyde Godfrey)
3 Lyde Mucegras
4 Lyde Saucey

MAUND:
- `---·---·` extent of Thornlaw Hundred in 1086
- `□□□□□` possible bounds of Maund District within above

1 Hope juxta Magene   7 Freen's Court (Mage)
2 Maund Bryan   8 Marden
3 Maund Aubin
4 Whitchurch Maund
5 Rosemaund
6 Nunnington (in Magarna)

PBR
9/88

Fig. 4. The district of Lyde and Maund
(Bruce Coplestone-Crow).

land between the Severn and the Wye as a lost province of the Cymry[17] and in the 19th century it was still possible to trace a Welsh linguistic boundary, which excluded east Herefordshire but embraced the Hereford basin.[18] During this period a vivid light is thrown upon the region immediately to the west of Hereford in the Llandaff charters, where petty kings abound who are eager to exploit Christian churchmen as the guardians of their patrimony, annexed from the decayed Roman state.[19] It is logical to conclude that a similar socio-political situation must have prevailed on the north and east sides of the Wye, but because of the later orientation of most of Herefordshire towards the English monarchy, few traditions of this era have been preserved. Thus the official documentary history of Herefordshire

begins in the mid-7th century with a local king, Merewahl, whose principal claim to fame is that he delivered Herefordshire into the hands of a Midland ruler – the king of Mercia.[20]

Long before this, there appears to have been a sub-kingdom or regional unit that focussed upon the Hereford basin. Its boundaries have been reconstructed and it seems to have been the successor to the territory surrounding the Roman town of Kenchester (*Magnis*). It has been christened *Lydas*, on the evidence of a mid-7th century charter (Fig. 4). In Domesday Book the Hereford basin was (to the east of the Wye) divided into two hundreds separated by the river Lugg – Cutsthorn (to the west) and *stepleset*, later Thornlow, (to the east). This division had its origins in a classic arrangement for land management in the Dark Ages – the multiple-estate – which is common elsewhere in England and widespread in Wales.[21] East of the Lugg was the king's estate, probably known as *Magana* and represented today in the place-names Maund and Marden, which ultimately derive from the Romano-British name for Kenchester – *Magnis*.[22] Whilst on the west was the church estate, which in *c*.675 belonged to the monastery at Wenlock although subsequently some of it came into the possession of the cathedral at Hereford, situated on the southern boundary of *Lydas*. Originally, it may have belonged to the British churchmen who served the Christian people of the region. In the reign of Henry I *Lydas/Magana* were reunited as the hundred of Grimsworth with its meeting place for the folk at the 'The Hundred Pit' enclosed by the *grim-wrasn* – Grim's ring or enclosure – on Credenhill.[23] The Iron Age hill-fort that had given its name to *Magnis* – *maen* – old Welsh 'stone/rock'. Archaeological work at Kenchester suggests the town was still occupied in the early 5th century, but following the pattern of hill-fort re-occupation in parts of south-western Britain, Credenhill may have been briefly brought into use again during the 5th century as a 'central or enclosed place' – hence its reappearance as a hundred meeting place in later centuries which, in some respects, restored the administrative unity to the *'regione que appellatur Lydas'*.[24]

The hundred – an administrative unit between the parish and the shire – survived until the early 20th century, although regularly reorganised in the Middle Ages and later. It frequently reflects earlier political or tribal arrangements.[25] The relationship between the Domesday hundreds of Thornlow and Cutsthorn (later united as Grimsworth) with the early districts of Lyde and Maund, which in turn have a strong connection, via the place-names *Maen – Magnis* – Maund – Marden, with Kenchester and ultimately Credenhill, seems to reflect administrative and political arrangements, which prevailed between the decline of Roman life at Kenchester in the early 5th century and the development of something English on the Hereford terrace in the late 7th century.

The people of Lyde and Maund, along with their western neighbours, were Christian – claiming continuity with the religion made universal in the Roman Empire by the Emperor Constantine in the early 4th century. Initially, the focus for the faithful was at Kenchester where Keith Ray has recently drawn attention to the fragments of artefacts of Christian origin, including a piece of a baptismal tank. It is also likely that the 'Ken' of the English name for *Magnis* (Kenchester) relates to the British priest or holy man who could be found in the Roman town perhaps long after its secular importance had declined.[26] Although the Wye appears to have been a boundary even in the Dark Ages – hence *Lydas* and Maund are confined to its northern side – there are, nevertheless, one or two clues from later ecclesiastical arrangements, which suggest that the river may have been less of an

impediment for travelling churchmen (*peregrini*) in earlier times. Today the dedications of the principal saint of Ergyng – St. Dyfrig (Dubricius) – are restricted to the south and west of the Wye, but in the early 16th century there was a chapel dedicated to him in Woolhope parish where the saint is said to have had a vision and performed many miracles. This is a rather late evidence but of similar significance, and dating from the early 14th century, is the revealing information that the church at Lugwardine also had extensive patronage across the Wye and was the mother church to a number of chapels including Hentland, where according to his *Life*, in the 6th or early 7th century, Dyfrig had a monastery. A substantial Roman site exists in the south-eastern corner of the parish of Lugwardine, which may have something to do with the unusual influence of this church whose dependencies seem to ignore the separation of Ergyng from English Herefordshire that occurred from the late 8th century onwards.[27] Perhaps before the arrival of the Mercian kings the region had been much more integrated.

Like their fellow churchmen in Ergyng, those in *Lydas* would have attached themselves to the local rulers, and through their generosity and desire for salvation would have acquired property on which churches and monasteries could be founded. The Mercian kings absorbed Herefordshire including *Lydas,* in the early 8th century, and the *Anglo-Saxon Chronicle* in 792 suggests that King Offa had a palace at Sutton in *Magana*.[28] It might be assumed, from evidence elsewhere in England, that there was an element of continuity in his choice. In Domesday Book much of the area remained in royal hands, but a number places – Sutton St. Michael and St. Nicholas, parts of Marden, Maund, Hinton, Felton, Thinghill – either belonged to the priests of St. Guthlac on Castle Green or had recently been lost by them.[29] As the monks of St.. Guthlac later claimed, they had previously been regarded as a royal demesne church and, from the evidence of Domesday, presumably served the king in the royal chapel at Sutton.[30] Although Hereford cathedral ultimately received a large part of *Lydas*, it was the older church of St. Guthlac that was more intimately connected with royalty, both the Mercians and presumably the people of *Lydas* before them (Fig. 5). Thus, even without the archaeological evidence for its early date, St. Guthlac's was endowed with property at the heart of *Lydas* in close proximity to a royal palace. If the post-conquest cartulary of the minster is to be believed, it also held churches and tithes at Bodenham, Burghope, Stoke Lacy, Ocle Pychard, Lugwardine, Bartestree, Mordiford, Larport, Yarkhill, Dormington, Little Cowarne, and Upper Lyde. This represents a great swathe of influence extending right across *Lydas* and beyond with Hereford (Castle Green) as its focal point. It certainly knocks the cathedral's patronage into a cocked hat and suggests that it must have been late on the scene – an interloper.[31]

The British church in the border survived until the mid-7th century when a new diocesan structure was imposed upon the lands west of the Severn Valley. The churchmen at *Lydas*, along with those at Leominster, Ledbury, Bromyard, Worcester and many other places in the region, were brought painlessly into the Roman church of the southern English.[32] This was associated in Herefordshire with increasing Mercian influence, especially in the north of the county around Leominster. Most of the knowledge about this process is derived from the *Life of St Milburga*, abbess of Wenlock and the daughter of Merewahl (*fl. c.*660), who was called king of the Magonsaete. Merewahl's title suggests he was connected with *Magana* but this was probably a recent connection as his name translates as 'border foreigner'. He was the son of the Mercian king, Penda, and, according to Joe Hillaby, his daughter Mildburg represented 'the advance guard of the new order', which ultimately led to the introduction of 'Roman ways' in his kingdom, in particular, the creation of a new diocese some-where between 680-90.[33]

South of Dinmore Hill progress may have been slower. Indeed, a laconic comment by Bishop Gilbert Foliot in the 12th century about

Fig. 5. View from Lyde Hill across the Lugg flood plain to Marden and Dinmore Hill – the heart of Lydas *(2006).*

Fig. 6. Ledbury Church seen across the fish-pond at Upper Hall – a property that anciently belonged to the religious community at Ledbury (2000).

variously described by Trefnant as *rex Britannie* and *Anglorum rex* – epitomising the mixed origins of his family and the people he ruled. Trefnant's claim helps to date the moment when the first bishops were endowed with their string of estates on the western flank of the Malverns.[35] Florence of Worcester refers to the earliest incumbents of the see as the bishops of the western *Hecani* and their names are known from an early list copied by William of Malmsbury from a manuscript at Malmsbury, which in turn had been copied from an ancient, but unplaced, stone. At Ledbury the early bishops of the western *Hecani* were comfortably close to their fellow bishops at Worcester serving the people of eastern *Hecani* (the Hwicce), beyond the Malverns, in the Severn Valley (Fig. 6).[36]

The Arrival of the Cathedral

By 803 the bishop's see was fixed at Hereford and, rather conveniently for the argument aired above, the charter that provides this date is concerned with settling a dispute between the bishops of Hereford and Worcester over two minsters, Beckford and Prestbury, located in the Severn Valley. As these belonged to Wulfheard, the bishop of Hereford, it strengthens the view that originally the bishops of the western Hecani had an eastern orientation and, as Florence of Worcester believed, were closely allied to the Hwicce. Significantly, the bishop of Hereford, also anciently, held Inkberrow in Worcestershire. The same charter of 803 acknowledges that there had been a 'church of Hereford in ancient days' – probably that on Castle Green.[37] The removal of the Roman bishop (hitherto domiciled at Ledbury) to Hereford, was made necessary by the activities of the Mercian kings. Aethelbald and Offa had firmly integrated the Welsh border into their kingdom and had extended their authority across the Wye, thus annexing, during the late 8th century, the northern part of Ergyng.[38] The new church at Hereford received a great deal of patronage in the conquered territories as well as estates in *Lydas*, which had previously belonged to Wenlock and earlier, to the British church. The

his predecessor at *Lidebiri* (Ledbury), suggests that the earliest Roman bishops of the area may have kept out of the way, settling to the lee of the Malverns in an area of Herefordshire linguistically English.[34] Significantly, most of the bishops' estates were to be found here in the Middle Ages and in 1394, when Bishop Trefnant was trying to defend his chase, which extended from Colwall to Cradley (to the north-east of Ledbury), he claimed that this considerable territory had been given to his predecessors by 'Mereduth' – 'the king of the whole of Herefordshire and parts round about'. 'Mereduth' is clearly Mildfrith, the son of Merewahl, brother of Mildburg, who ruled in *c*.690 and is recruited to add credence to the association of the cathedral with St. Ethelbert in the *Vita S. Ethelberti*. He is

Fig. 7. Hereford Cathedral: intruded by the Mercian kings into an earlier religious landscape (2006).

bishop also brought with him the gifts of Mildfrith in the east of the diocese.

The new cathedral was presumably built fairly close to the river and perhaps, following Silas Taylor's observations in the mid-17th century, nearer to the modern Cathedral School. This involved a major reorganisation of the settlement and the new 'town' was laid out on a grid pattern that extended to the north and, possibly, to the west across the morass of the King's Ditch. In the early 9th century the cathedral and the new town were enclosed with a ditch. Although he died in 796, there can be little doubt that this major piece of town planning had been inaugurated by King Offa (Aethelbald being the other possibility). From the beginning, cathedral and fortress were conceived together, as they would have been for Charlemagne, Offa's great contemporary on the continent (Fig. 7).[39]

To the east of the cathedral – across the watery outflow of the holy well – was a graveyard, set aside from the community that had now become the new Mercian town. Ron Shoesmith's excavations on Castle Green in 1973 suggest strongly that there

Fig. 8. The condition of Castle Cliffe before the 1973 excavations started. Some of the concrete revetments are stored above the cliff.

Fig. 9. The 1973 excavation on Castle Green.

Top left: Schoolchildren from Haywood school working on site

Above: A series of early skeletons

Left: Foundations of what was probably a pre-conquest building
(Ron Shoesmith)

were Christian burials, taking place near the southern tip of the Green, at least a century before the foundation of the cathedral Fig. 8). This makes the cemetery one of the earliest in use in England and, if it was associated with a church on the Green, even more special (Fig. 9). There were certainly two small buildings here. One of them, built of stone, was the focus for many of the burials, and John Blair suggests that it might have been a mausoleum for an important person. Nearby, slightly raised on a low mound, was a timber building, which was subsequently rebuilt after the Conquest as a stone church dedicated to St. Martin (Fig 10 & Pl. 1).[40] It seems unlikely that an important burial ground should have been left without caretakers, and thus a monastery or church adjacent to the burials seems essential. There is plenty of room to the north and east, where parch marks have revealed a complex pattern of ditches, postholes and burials, some of which, of course, must be associated with the later castle. The whole

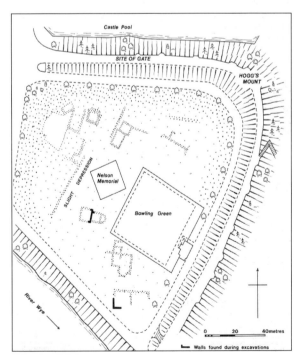

Fig. 10. Plan of the parch marks revealed on Castle Green in 1975 (Ron Shoesmith).

complex, raised up on its gravel cliff and probably enclosed on the north and east, was a typical site for an early monastery. Moreover, below it was a spring, which continued to have a reputation as a holy well until the early 20th century. It is difficult not to see this well as the baptismal focus for the earliest Christians occupying the Hereford basin.[41] Soon after 792 it received its dedication to St. Ethelbert, the King of the East Angles, who was murdered by Offa at Sutton, and whose body was probably buried in the ancient burial ground known simply to a later chronicler as Fernley.[42] With the foundation of the new cathedral, the saint's bones were re-interred in the new church, which received his name as part of its dedication (Fig. 11). St. Ethelbert may not have been the first East Anglian to be buried on Castle Green. This priv-

ilege probably belongs to St. Guthlac whose body arrived about half a century earlier.

St. Guthlac of Crowland was closely associated with Aethelbald, king of Mercia (716-57) who in c.740 crossed the Wye and extended Mercian authority into Ergyng. Before becoming king of Mercia, Aethelbald had spent two years with Guthlac in his solitary retreat amidst the Fens and even after the saint's death in c.715, Aethelbald visited his hermitage to receive reassurance from him (Fig. 11). St. Guthlac was himself descended from the Mercian royal house and from the age of fifteen (c.685) he spent nine years on military adventures. Later he was tormented by demons, presumably his old enemies, who spoke the British language, so it is likely that between c.685-94 he was campaigning on the Welsh border. His expeditions were a

Fig. 11. St Ethelbert's Well – the rededication ceremony in May 1978 – the anniversary of the murder of King Ethelbert (Len White).

prelude to those of Aethelbald, nearly 50 years later, that created the political framework of the southern Marches as we know it today. Aethelbald's grandfather, Eowa, was the brother of Merewalh whilst Guthlac was also, presumably, a distant kinsman. A *Life* of St. Guthlac was kept in the library at Leominster, which had been founded by Merewahl, and prayers to the saint are found in the Anglo-Saxon histories.[43] Guthlac's youthful campaigns on the border would have taken place in the time of Merchelm or Mildfrith – Merewalh's sons. Mildfrith, as has been shown, was a benefactor of the earliest bishops. These connections make it very likely that the cult of St. Guthlac – together with part of his body – were introduced into Hereford in Aethelbald's time. As a saint, whose desire for isolation was reminiscent of the life style of the early saints of Wales, he would have been very comfortable with Castle Green and its close connections with an eremitic church.[44] The presence of a shrine to an important Mercian saint makes it all the more likely that the graveyard was accompanied by a community of priests who obviously also benefited from Aethebald's campaigns – obtaining, somewhat earlier than the cathedral, some important properties in Ergyng, including the Dubrician centre of Moccas where the saint had founded a monastery. Alternatively, of course, as a British monastery they may have enjoyed some of these properties before.

It could be argued that St. Guthlac and Aethelbald were the founders of the church on Castle Green – the radio-carbon dating for the earliest burials would fit into this timeframe. However, recent fieldwork close to Hereford has indicated that there were several other 'open' Christian burial grounds within a few miles of Castle Green – perhaps, 'half a dozen cemeteries in a ring around Hereford' according to Tim Hoverd. One of these, at Ashgrove in Sutton, was

close to the site of Offa's putative palace and seems to have contained Christians and, possibly, pagans, buried side by side (Fig. 12).[45] The status of the Castle Green graveyard, and its relationship to these cemeteries, is difficult to ascertain, but Aethelbald's patronage certainly elevated it into a different league, making it one of the famous 'resting places of the saints', lists of which were regularly circulated in the Old English period.

Fig. 12. A disused gravel pit 'at the top of Sutton Upper Field' where 'Saxon' burials were discovered in 1798 (2006).

Thus in 803 the new cathedral and its bishop found themselves sharing the Hereford terrace with a more ancient foundation. It too had royal connexions and regularly claimed that it was supported by royal alms and possessed prebendaries, dignities and parishes. In other words, it was a mother church of other churches – a minster establishment, manned by secular priests who shared the common fund derived from its accumulated properties and churches. The burial ground on Castle Green continued to be popular and seems, notwithstanding the status of the new cathedral, to have absorbed the departed of a large proportion of the inhabitants of the burgeoning Mercian town. Only when radio-carbon dates have been established for the burials recently found near the west end of the cathedral, will it be possible to say for certain that St.

Fig. 13. Looking across the fishponds to the site of Buca's minster at Acton Beauchamp (2006).

Guthlac's did not retain the total loyalty of the people of Hereford as a place of burial in the Old English period.

A Royal Place

The establishment of the cathedral, the re-organisation of the town and the creation of the defensive circuit, through the intervention of the Mercian kings, made Hereford a royal centre. Although the tribal name Magonsaete is occasionally used to describe the people of the southern Marches until the eve of the Norman Conquest, its local dynasty, already closely associated with the Mercians, was eclipsed. It seems likely that the royal palace at Sutton, obliquely referred to in 792, may well at some point have been replaced by a royal hall in Hereford itself. Recent archaeology at Sutton and Marden has provided some tantalising evidence for the putative palace.[46]

One of the most significant aspects of Hereford in later centuries is its role as a royal

place. It became a 'burh' in the 10th century, a focus of resistance against the Welsh in the mid-11th century, an accounting centre in Domesday, the site of a royal castle and, in the early Middle Ages, a chartered trading centre with a royal new town, which was governed by royal bailiffs. Moreover, it had become a shire town around the early 11th century, where public assemblies took place and, throughout the later Middle Ages, a place where the Marcher courts were held. Finally, in the 16th and 17th centuries, it was used regularly for meetings of the Council in the Marches and was defended as a Royalist stronghold during the Civil War. This royal status appears to be of great antiquity and must date from at least the Mercian period. As John Blair points out, Hereford is one of those places, descended from an earlier monastic site, where secular interest quickly became involved and where the church never had a clear primacy especially when the crown began to develop a royal fortress policy. It is clear that the

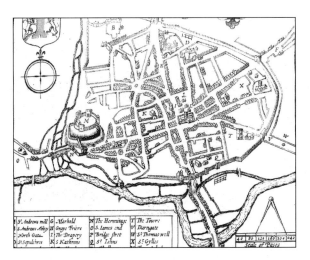

*Fig. 14. John Speed's plan of Northampton,
1610. St Peter's church (S)
is sited below the castle (M).
The royal hall was immediately to the east.*

town became a place where a royal focus or administrative headquarters was added to a major religious centre.[47] Within Hereford there would have been a royal hall or, perhaps less formally, at least a place where the king or his officers could expect hospitality. This is most likely to be found where its successor was situated in the Middle Ages – on Castle Green.

Aethelbald was unpopular with strict churchmen of his time, such as St. Boniface, because of the secular demands he put upon minsters for hospitality, fortress construction and bridge building. He also rewarded his followers with smaller religious houses, which became 'family minsters' – places of residence, retirement or simply a resort for occasional material or spiritual nourishment. In 727 a small minster at Acton Beauchamp in east Herefordshire was given to Aethelbald's ancient retainer, Buca. It appears to have remained a religious centre, albeit now in lay hands (Fig. 13). It would seem possible that St. Guthlac's was treated in a similar fashion but subject to royal control.[48]

The lack of direct documentary evidence means that what follows is very speculative but may some day be either confirmed or confounded by further excavations on Castle Green. The

excavations at Northampton between 1980-82 revealed two royal halls dating from the late 8th and early 9th centuries.[49] They provide a context for speculation upon the royal presence in Hereford. The first high status timber hall (29.7 x 8.6 m.) would fit easily into the unexcavated areas of Castle Green. Significantly, the Northampton hall was placed immediately to the east of an old minster dedicated to St. Peter – a dedication shared by many important churches in this period, including St. Guthlac's, where it could be the primary dedication.[50] At Northampton, to the east of the hall, there was another church dedicated to St. Gregory which, like St. Martin's that was later situated in the centre of Castle Green, makes no documentary appearance until the middle of the 12th century, but is nevertheless located in the midst of an extensive early graveyard. One of the features of early minster sites is the multiplication of churches or oratories within the precinct (Fig. 14). Another, more concrete connection with Northampton, relates to its name *hamtun* – the 'north' prefix being added in the 12th century. In the famous charter issued by Bishop Robert of Lorraine in 1085, which made a grant to Roger de Lacy of the bishop's manor of Holme Lacy in return for the service of two knights, the bishop reserves for the benefit of his tenants at Hereford and King's Hampton access to the woods at Holme Lacy.[51] King's Hampton is clearly next to Hampton Bishop, close to Hereford and not far from Holme Lacy, but it has disappeared out of modern usage.

Looking at a map of Hereford and its medieval parishes suggests immediately that the small and fragmented parishes of the city were annexed from surrounding rural ones (Fig. 15).[52] All the parish churches of the city appear to be Norman foundations and were inserted into an existing parochial landscape. The church of All Saints, in the Norman new town, for example, was a chapelry of St. Martin's across Wye bridge and presumably enjoyed part of its extensive parish.[53] St. Peter's – at the other end of the Norman market place – on the other hand, was

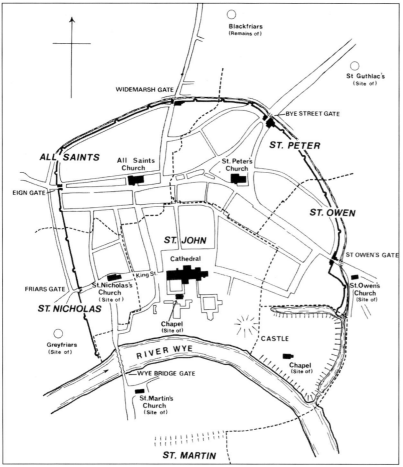

Fig. 15. The city parishes and their boundaries (Ron Shoesmith).

late 11th century, intermingled with those of the cathedral.[55] Collectively this area may have been the King's Hampton. Gover, Mawer and Stenton argued in 1933 that the 'Old English *hamtun* carried something of the sense of the modern "home farm" or in more general terms of a central residence'. Like Northampton the King's Hampton 'was a royal residence and estate at which were rendered the dues payable by the men of the folk – the provincia or regio – settled around it'.[56]

One of St. Guthlac's problems as an ancient minster in the eyes of recent interpreters is that it lacked a *parochia* – an extended parish, often with satellite chapels, for which the minster acted as a mother church. St. Guthlac's certainly held extensive estates, many of them lying in areas that suggest royal patronage at an early date. Two 12th century charters provide some indication of the extensive patrimony of the minster. St. Peter and St. Owen in the city, Holme Lacy, Ocle Pychard, Mordiford, Bartestree, Sutton St. Michael, Sutton St. Nicholas, Avebury, Monnington, Moccas, Presteigne, Felton, Little Cowarne, Edwin Loach, Dormington, Marden and Load in Somerset were all chapelries of St. Guthlac. In addition it received tithes from Staunton on Wye, Risbury, Humber, Wheathill (?), Butterley, Street, Weobley, Burghope, Bodenham, Maund, Stoke Lacy, Weston Beggard, Kempley, Gatterhope, Oxenhall, Lugwardine, Wacton, Rosemaund and Upper Lyde. Much of this seems to derive from the patronage of the de Lacys and their tenants, but there may, even so, be a substantial element of continuity with the pre-Conquest patrimony of the minster. The monks of the post-Conquest

founded by Walter de Lacy and started life as a chapel of St. Guthlac's, but its parish appears to have been extracted from that of Hampton Bishop.[54] This provides a useful clue; for the precinct of the castle – ex-parochial in the Middle Ages – is surrounded by the small parish of St. Owen (another Norman foundation), which again may have been cut out of Hampton Bishop. Thus, Hampton Bishop originally surrounded Castle Green and it follows that the King's Hampton was likely to have been situated here. It was so called to distinguish it from Hampton Bishop, the focus of the parish, some two miles away. Logically, the King's *hamtun* would have been situated on Castle Green with lands adjoining it in Bartonsham, Eign and Litley, all places where St. Guthlac's owned property in the priory of St. Guthlac were clearly conscious of the antiquity of their foundation and a spurious charter in a 15th century hand makes a clumsy attempt at recreating the parochial rights of the monastery, adding further daughter churches, several in the Welsh parts of Herefordshire, and even naming the prebendal estates. All this evidence suggests that albeit St. Guthlac's lacked a compact *parochia* it had once been a mother church with cathedral-like authority over lowland Herefordshire.[57]

But little of this land, on the basis of the Domesday information where it lay scattered and fragmented, could be connected together as a coherent territory. This is also a problem with the cathedral estates, as has already been noted. Much of St. Guthlac's estate was encroached upon by laymen/women, perhaps as a result of the stresses of the Welsh wars during Edward the Confessor's reign. But again, at this time, the lands of the bishop, as well as those of the nun-minster at Leominster, were also being exploited for the war effort. In Domesday, it is recorded that William had restored the bishop's estates, but he still held those of Leominster, whilst St. Guthlac's was suffering another phase of lay predation. It had to wait until the mid-12th century for Bishop Robert de Bethune and Hugh de Lacy to partially restore its fortunes.

If St. Guthlac's was the primary church of the Hereford terrace, why did it not have an extensive parish like St. Helen's in Worcester and St. Mary's in Shrewsbury?[58] As befits the late arrival of the bishop, the cathedral held sway over the small parish of St. John, which included the immediate precincts and some scattered areas, presumably added to it at a later date in a rather arbitrary way. There was never a parish church of St. John and the services for the parishioners were traditionally held in the north transept of the cathedral. It has already been suggested that the city parishes of All Saints, St. Peter, St. Owen and St. Nicholas were cut out of the surrounding rural parishes and, taken together, they could be regarded as St. Guthlac's *parochia* extending to some 1,653 acres. The Mercian kings may have created or acknowledged the existence of this large parish, which was subsequently broken up in the immediate post-Conquest period when the city was provided with the new churches listed above. This would coincide with the nadir of the old minster's fortunes.

There remains another ambiguous administrative unit, which appears to be of considerable antiquity – the Liberty of the City of Hereford.[59] In the late 19th century this contained 4,820 acres and as such defined the administrative boundary of the city right up until the demise of the Hereford District Council in the early 1990s (Fig.16). It is still marked by boundary stones, mostly 19th century in date but some much earlier, and in all periods of history it has been strenuously defended. Throughout the Middle Ages and beyond, inquisitions were held at strategic places so as to remind the rural inhabitants of the Liberty that they were under the jurisdiction of royal bailiffs and later the magistrates of the chartered city. The Liberty ignores the boundaries of the surrounding rural parishes and follows, where possible, topographical features – the line of the Roman road on the north-west, the Lugg Rhea and the eastern escarpment overlooking the Lugg flood plain and, to the north of the Wye, it follows the Withy and Newton brook. Only to the west does it zigzag along a negotiated boundary with Breinton. Earlier antiquarians, with no documentary support, suggested that it represented a *territorium* given by King Offa to the bishop, in expiation for the murder of King Ethelbert.[60] The flaw in this argument is that the bishop was never involved in its jurisdiction which, in the Middle Ages at least, remained in the hands of the king's representatives in Hereford – the royal bailiffs. The church of Hereford certainly owned substantial estates within the Liberty and some supported prebendaries, but its boundaries failed to coincide with those of the deanery, under the jurisdiction of the cathedral, which was mainly to the west of the Wye.

It is possible to speculate, therefore, that the Liberty represents an early royal estate, which subsequently became the hundred of the city, for

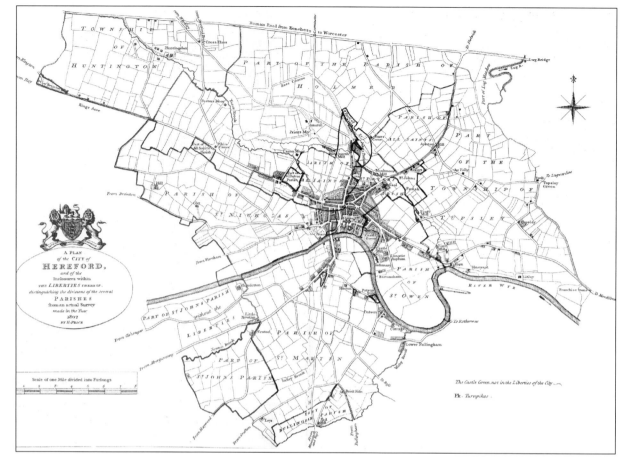

Fig. 16. The liberty of the city of Hereford surveyed by Henry Price in 1802.

which St. Guthlac's was the *matrix ecclesia*. This may have been its lost *parochia* – the royal jurisdiction over the Liberty survived, but the spiritual authority of St. Guthlac's disappeared, along with many of its possessions, in the early 11th century.

A further indication of the royal presence in Hereford can possibly be detected in the Bartonsham farm, which lies to the south-east of Castle Green and was approached from the city in the early Middle Ages by 'the Green Way of the King'.[61] The *bertun,* or 'corn farm reserved for the lord's use', is usually assumed to have been part of the demesne lands of the cathedral, but it may originally have been the king's manor and in the 12th century some of the lands here belonged to St. Guthlac (Fig. 17).[62] At Gloucester, the royal palace at

Kingsholm was surrounded by the royal estate of Barton Regis which, like the Liberty at Hereford, formed a discrete hundred.[63] But at Gloucester the palace was detached from the city, occupying the ramparts of a first century Roman fort, serving, no doubt, the same purpose as the enclosing *vallum* of the monastic precinct on Castle Green. Kingsholm had also been used as a burial ground before it became a royal palace. Some evidence of the continuity of royal influence occurs after 1066, when William fitzOsbern had all his revenues from estates in Herefordshire, Worcestershire and Gloucestershire accounted in Hereford. But this was in his new castle, which had apparently metamorphosed from the earlier king's residence within the *vallum* of St. Guthlac's minster.

Fig. 17. Bartonsham Farm (2006) – gave its name to a prebendal estate in the 13th century but earlier may have been the 'king's barton' attached to the royal hall.

From Royal Monastery to Castle

Burials continued to take place on Castle Green until the early 12th century when St. Guthlac's was totally rebuilt in the northern suburbs of the city as a priory of Gloucester abbey. After this move, the cathedral close became the principal graveyard for the city and the adjoining country parishes. At the date of re-foundation, the minster and graveyard were described as being inconveniently located within the bailey of the royal castle, founded soon after 1066. The desecration of ancient minsters at the Norman Conquest by the building of castles was a widespread phenomenon. The royal castle at Worcester occupied a large portion of the cathedral close and apparently encircled the old minster of St. Peter's within its bailey. Similarly, at Warwick the old minster of St. Mary and its precincts were completely destroyed by the new castle, whilst at Northampton the

castle is squeezed to the north-west of St. Peter's. But here, the proximity of the earlier and now abandoned Anglo-Saxon halls suggests there was an element of continuity in the site chosen for the castle, which is paralleled at Hereford.[64] The pious Normans, renowned for the respect for the reformed church, were not being predatory in exploiting minster sites for castles, but in many cases were simply laying claim to royal places and expressing this ownership in a more forthright manner – in towers and battlements.[65]

Royal interest in St. Guthlac's intensified in the 10th and 11th centuries. Mercian kingship languished in the early 9th century in the face of the Viking onslaught and was replaced by West Saxon over-lordship. East Anglia and the East Midlands were absorbed into the Danelaw and although West Mercia was remote from the areas of Scandinavian settlement, the Vikings used the

Severn to penetrate deeply into an area rich in monasteries. By the late 9th century, with Alfred on the throne, West Mercia was the responsibility of earl Aethelred, who married Alfred's daughter, Aethelflaed.[66] In 893 Aethelred called out the levies from the West Mercian 'burhs', referring specifically to those 'west of the Severn, together with a section of the Welsh'.[67] The latter must refer to Hereford and suggests that the first phase of the defences, excavated in Cantilupe Street between 1972 and 1975, were in existence three years before the establishment of similar

Fig. 18. Cantilupe Street defences showing signs of Aethelflaed's timber palisade with the later stone wall behind (Ron Shoesmith).

urban fortifications at Worcester which are dated to 896, though documentary evidence is not always precise (Fig. 18). Aethelflaed, 'the Lady of the Mercians', was a compulsive 'burh' builder, extending the system established by her father in Wessex to English Mercia.[68] As the Cantilupe Street excavations demonstrated, the enclosure of St. Guthlac's precinct and its integration into the town of Hereford took place at this moment. The Mercian defences were extended to enclose a large area of land around Castle Street – the main eastern thoroughfare out of the city – which could then be used to gather the local levies or to provide an emergency camping ground for the folk of the region that was soon to be organised as the shire.[69] The zone to the north of the road remained open ground throughout the Middle Ages and became the dairy of the canons – hence the original name for St. John Street – *milklone*. An additional reason for the extension of the ramparts around St. Guthlac's was perhaps, to defend the royal centre and, given Aethelflaed's legendary piety, the holy

relics of two East Anglian saints – St. Guthlac and St. Ethelbert (Fig. 19).

However, the Viking raids brought new pressures upon the ancient minsters all over England. Not only were they looted and destroyed by the enemy, but their protectors also expected them to play their part in the life and death struggle. Alfred and his successors secularised religious estates to provide resources for the war effort and St. Guthlac's, endowed at an early date and closely identified with the defunct Mercian dynasty, was especially vulnerable. The fragmented character of the minster's estates in *Domesday Book*, often in the hands of laymen, and its apparent lack of a *parochia*, was probably the result of West Saxon predations, which continued beyond the Norman Conquest. Hereford's defences – built initially by Ethelred and Aethelflaed in earth and timber – were reconstructed in stone by Edward the Elder or Athelstan before *c*.930. The informal hospitality expected by the Mercian rulers from their religious houses

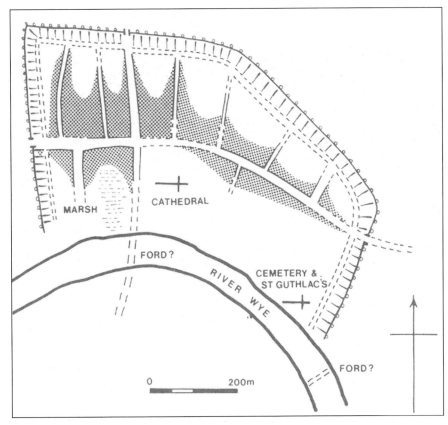

Fig. 19. Plan of the extended defences in the early 10th century, now enclosing St Guthlac's and possibly, the royal hall (Ron Shoesmith).

Castle Green. Although Kingsholm at Gloucester was regularly visited by Edward the Confessor, and on one occasion used as a crowning centre, visits to Hereford are unrecorded. The main attraction of Kingsholm for Edward was apparently the proximity of the Forest of Dean and the opportunities it provided for hunting. However, Hereford was also a favoured base for hunting, for *Domesday Book* records that before 1066 the citizens were bound to attend the king to 'stall game' in the woodland of Treville Forest, to the south-west of the city, where the men of the royal 'ton' (Kingstone) brought the produce of the hunt back to Hereford. Treville was the most northerly of the royal game reserves, which existed on the west side of the Wye, above the Forest of Dean. Their names are recorded after the Conquest – Penyard Chase, Harewood, Aconbury, Haywood and Treville. Presumably, Edward, on his visits to Kingsholm, occasionally found himself after a day's hunting close to Hereford where, it can be supposed, he spent the night in the royal palace on Castle Green.

Domesday provides further evidence for the existence of a royal hall at Hereford. In the early Middle Ages a serjeantry was attached to the royal manor at Marden, which required its holder to measure 'the ditches of Hereford Castle and oversee the workmen'. Colvin believes this was a certain Stephen, who held a virgate of land in Marden in *Domesday Book*. Significantly, Stephen's predecessor before 1066 was Alfward, a substantial landowner,

probably became something more permanent for the West Saxon 'burh' builders. Alfred turned Abingdon abbey into a royal residence, whilst at Westminster a royal palace was squeezed in beside the ancient minster at 'Kingsbury'.[70]

Although the West Saxon kings rarely visited Mercia, it seems likely that Aetheflaed used Hereford as a base for her attack upon the Welsh king's palace at Llangorse, and her nephew, King Athelstan, signed a treaty with the Welsh at Hereford in *c*.930. The new defences no doubt impressed the Welsh princes who would also have remembered that in 914 the men of the 'burh' had driven the Vikings from Ergyng and rescued the Welsh bishop of that region. The meeting could have taken place in the open, perhaps in the cathedral, or even in a putative hall adjoining the royal minster on freeman and thane of Oda, earl of the Hwiccas and a benefactor of the royal monastery at Deerhurst. Alfward lost most of his land after 1066, but still paid William 40d. for unidentified privileges at Leominster. It is just possible that Alfward was caretaker of the royal hall at Hereford before 1066 and Stephen was his Norman successor both in terms of land ownership and office.[71]

Aethelflaed was very concerned to enhance the religious importance of the West Midland 'burhs' sensing, perhaps, that something of the earlier prestige and enthusiasm of the Mercian church had been lost during the struggle against the Vikings. At Gloucester she founded a new minster church, next to the old minster of St. Peter, bringing the body of St. Oswald, her ancestor, from Northumberland. Something similar, but less well documented, appears to have occurred at Chester and Shrewsbury. This has led to the suggestion that Aethelflaed also brought the relics of St. Guthlac from Crowland to Hereford's Castle Green. The conquest of East Anglia by her brother, Edward, would have given Aethelflaed the opportunity to recover the bodies of saints hitherto inaccessible, being in regions occupied by the pagan Vikings.[72] Since St. Guthlac's makes its first documentary appearance in the late 10th century and appears, because of its scattered estates and lack of a *parochial,* to be anachronistic, this view has some credibility. However, there is little documentary support and it flies in the face of the archaeological evidence and the early date given to the 'saints resting places', which implies that St. Guthlac's relics were in Hereford by the mid-9th century. Moreover, Edward did not secure a treaty with the Danes of Cambridge and East Anglia until 921 and Aethelflaed died the following year, providing very little time for the translation of St. Guthlac's relics.[73] St. Oswald's body was transferred to Gloucester in 906, according to the *Anglo Saxon Chronicle*, but even here the new minster was added to a graveyard already in use in the mid-9th century and, like Hereford, there

is a strong possibility that there was already a chapel or mausoleum attached to the graveyard.[74] Similarly, at Shrewsbury, there is no firm documentary evidence that the cult of St. Alkmund, a Northumbrian saint, was established by Aethelflaed and it is more likely to have an early 9th-century origin. Steven Bassett believes that St. Alkmund's was one of three churches that formed an early 8th-century monastic complex in the centre of Shrewsbury, with St. Chad's as the 'head minster'. This arrangement seems very similar to Hereford, except that here the cathedral took the place of St. Chad's.[75] There is also no suggestion that Aethelflaed created a new minster at Worcester, where the cathedral was again surrounded by a cluster of early churches, which may have formed a similar monastic focus. Aethelflaed was not, it seems, the founder of St. Guthlac's, although it is still possible that she may have improved its endowments at the same time as encroaching upon its precinct.

The inclusion of the minster within the new military earthworks certainly suggests that St. Guthlac's was an institution of high status, and this is confirmed in two documents which refer to it in the late 10th and early 11th centuries. In the first, of *c.*975, a Shropshire thegn called Wulfgeat left half a pound in pence (silver coins) to St. Guthlac and a similar sum to the cathedral. St. Guthlac's takes precedence in the will over half a dozen other West Midland minsters. Similarly, in the early 11th century, a local thegn called Leofwine purchased an estate at Mansell in Herefordshire, with the cognisance of the two communities – ' St. Ethelbert's and St. Guthlac's'. It is possible that this new status was either the result of recent royal patronage or simply reflects the veneration felt by locals for an ancient establishment that had hitherto gone undocumented.[76]

The meeting between the Welsh and Athelstan at Hereford in *c.*930 reflects upon the growing importance of the city as the capital of the southern Marchland. In the 10th century it became a shire town with a mint and, almost

Fig. 20. The eastern end of Castle Street and the site of the corn market, probably established before the Conquest at the entrance to the precinct of St. Guthlac on the right (2006).

certainly, a market. The use of the Old English term 'port' in the *Anglo-Saxon Chronicle*, *Domesday Book* and locally in the 'Port Fields' (adjoining the town) and the 'Port Way' (approaching the town) provides confirmation for this.[77] The earliest markets, it has been assumed, took place to the north of the cathedral in an area that subsequently developed into the medieval close. This would have been much more spacious if, as seems likely, the early cathedral was closer to the river. After the Conquest the principal markets and fairs of the town were transferred to the Norman 'new town' – High Town – where an equally large market place, flanked by the churches of All Saints and St. Peter, was established by William fitzOsbern with the collaboration of the bishop.[78] The cathedral close became the principal graveyard for the city in the mid-

12th century, but appears to have retained some of its market functions, albeit these were increasingly incongruous. Bishop Mascal (1404-16) complained that it was regularly used as a cattle market and a threshing floor, and in 1389 the Dean and Chapter sought a royal license to enclose it with gates. However, remembering their ancient rights of ingress and egress to what had been the main thoroughfare of the city, the townsmen rioted and broke open the new gates.[79] Their rights to use the close as a public open space were established in perpetuity and Hereford's close was never really enclosed as was the case at Norwich.

Remarkably, something of the great Anglo-Saxon market place survived at the eastern end of Castle Street in front of the great gate of the castle (Fig. 20). Presumably as a result of the dispute about commercial activities in the close, a royal commission was established in 1395 to inquire into certain buildings erected by tenants of the Dean and Chapter on land adjoining the moat and bridge of the castle 'where the corn market has long been held'.[80] The corn market was presumably one of the most important markets in the city and was held here, no doubt by ancient prescription. The post-Conquest developments in Hereford made Castle Street a *cul-de-sac* and it is most unlikely that a new market would have been established in this out-of-the-way place in the early Middle Ages. Before the Conquest, however, this was at the eastern end of the great market place that stretched across the cathedral close towards the east gate of the city, now lost beneath Hogg's Mount. Detailed maps also suggest that Castle Street was much broader, especially on its north side, where there remained extensive gardens. This market place seems to acknowledge the pre-eminence of the cathedral which, after the Conquest, was the patron of the great St. Ethelbert's fair held in May – but there is an alternative possibility.

Like much else in early Hereford, in default of firm documentary evidence, the prime movers in the pre-Conquest city are usually regarded as being the king or the bishop – the importance of St. Guthlac's is often forgotten. If the focus of the ancient market place had always been where it still lay in 15th century – below the castle gate – this would previously have given direct access to the precincts of St. Guthlac's and to the putative royal palace. There is one further clue – when, in the mid-12th century, St. Guthlac's was re-founded as a regular Benedictine monastery in the northern suburbs of the city, its full dedication was to St. Peter, St. Paul and St. Guthlac.[81] The two additional dedications could be post-Conquest, but

it is equally likely, given the frequent use of these two primary saints for minster establishments, that this was the full dedication of the ancient minster in the Old English period. After all, St. Ethelbert's cathedral was also dedicated to St. Mary, but this was also rarely used before the Middle Ages. Significantly, throughout Britain, St. Peter and St. Paul dedications are often associated with churches adjoining early market places, some perhaps established as early as the 8th century.[82] Thus, when Aethelred and Aethelflaed extended the 'burh' defences of Hereford in the late 10th century, they may also have had in mind the protection of an existing market place, or possibly, as at Gloucester, next to St. Oswald's, a new market place, the preservation of which was essential during the struggle with the Vikings.[83]

In 1999 several trenches were dug to the south of the Castle House Hotel, between the building and the Castle Pool. There were surfaces and structures here associated with Chester-type ware dating from the mid-10th to the mid-11th centuries. One of the buildings investigated contained a loom and had been burnt down, leaving 13 loom weights *in situ* (Pl. 2). A pit containing fragments of pottery also provided seeds of bread wheat and other cereals. Possible traces of the eastern continuation of Castle Street, were found underneath Castle House, leaving the structures described above between the road and the precinct of St Guthlac. This evidence suggests that far from being a remote backwater, this area adjoining the minster, possibly, at its 'fore-gate', was the hub of commercial activity in the pre-conquest town. Indeed, the earliest phase of the road surface detected here, running towards the castle, may have originally provided access to the minster although subsequently being reconstructed as the entrance to the castle.[84]

CHAPTER III

Royalty : The Medieval Castle

Ralph's Castle?

Domesday Book suggests that during the Welsh Wars, fought during the last decades of the Old English rule, the patrimony of St. Guthlac's suffered heavily not only from the direct damage of war but more frequently from the predations of laymen and women who secured grants of church land, presumably in return for contributions to the war effort. Land of St. Guthlac's at Whitney and *Westelet* were said to have been laid waste, whilst several estates had been acquired by a noble woman called Leofled. Its most valuable possession at Pembridge in the Arrow valley – worth £16 *per annum* – had been 'wrongfully' taken by Earl Godwin and his son Harold. This was only the tip of the iceberg, and a detailed analysis of the lands held by Roger de Lacy, Nigel the Doctor and Hugh the Donkey after 1066 would certainly indicate further losses, which are not directly recorded.[85] Edward the Confessor gave all the wrong signals by granting the priests of St. Ethelbert sake and soke over all their lands on the eve of appointing Walter of Lorraine, his wife's chaplain, bishop of Hereford in *c.*1060.[86] No such protection for its lands was granted to St. Guthlac's. Overtly the greatest humiliation for St. Guthlac was the encroachment of the first Norman castle upon its precinct – an event which has been traditionally associated with Ralph of the 'Timid', son of Drogo, Count of the Vexin (between Normandy and the kingdom of France),

who was Edward the Confessor's nephew. He was probably created earl of Hereford in *c.*1052, replacing Swein Godwinson, Harold's brother, who was exiled in that year.[87]

The presence of a castle in Hereford before *c.*1067 is by no means certain, albeit it has been accepted as orthodoxy by most local, and many academic, historians of the period.[88] The *Anglo Saxon Chronicle* always refers to 'a castle' (1051) or 'the castle' (1052) and a little later to 'Pentecost's castle' (1052), which J.H. Round, many years ago, identified as Ewyas Harold castle.[89] However, when events focussed on Hereford in 1055, and Gruffydd ap Llyewelyn and Aelfgar of Mercia defeated Earl Ralph and the local levies outside the city, there is no mention of a castle, notwithstanding that the defeated forces took refuge in the city. John of Worcester (also known as 'Florence') provides an extended account of the disaster, with much local detail, but still does not mention a castle. Moreover, when Earl Harold arrived and took command of the situation, his first consideration was to repair the 'burh' defences 'with gates and bars and with a broad deep ditch'.[90] He reacted as a true servant of the Old English state and appears to have spurned the novelty of castles, which were particularly associated at that time with the perfidious French. The gravel bank, hastily thrown over the decayed Saxon defences, located in Victoria Street during the 1968 excavations, may well

Fig. 21. Whitecross – a mile to the west of the city and, notwithstanding its association with bishop Charlton (1361-69) as a plague cross, seems likely to have marked the site of the battle of Hereford in 1055 (Havergal).

Red Book version of the *Brut y Tywysogyon* (*The Chronicle of the Princes*) where, following the defeat of Raph's army outside the city, 'Gruffydd closely pursued them to the fortress (*y gaer*); and he entered therein and he pillaged the fortress (*gaer*) and destroyed it and burned the town (*y dref*)'. John Williams ab Ithel suggested in 1860 that the use of *gaer* and *tref* was to distinguish between the castle and the town.[92] Thus, John Lloyd's reading of the events in 1055 was 'the castle was taken with a rush ere its terrified inmates had time to rise from their meal'. For this dramatic scene he also had the benefit of the *Brenhineddy Saesson* (*Chronicle of the Saxons*), perhaps the least reliable of the Welsh chronicles, which states 'they were driven in flight as far as Hereford, being slaughtered the while: and whilst they were at their meat, they attacked the fortress and destroyed it and burned it and pillaged it'.[93] Of course, Hereford in 1055 was both a fortress and a town – a 'burh' and a borough – as Harold acknowledged by building the 'broad deep ditch'. Although archaeological evidence suggests the wall was down in Victoria Street, on the east side of the city, in Cantilupe Street, it was most likely standing high and indeed, since its construction in the early 10th century, had been occasionally repaired. The Peniarth version of the *Brut y Tywysogyon* seems to grasp that Hereford was both a fortress and a town and the modern translation renders the key sentence as 'Gruffydd pursued them within the walls of Hereford, and there he massacred them and destroyed the walls and burned the town'.[94] Clearly, the most straightforward interpretation of these events excludes the presence of a castle. Indeed, the bravado of the defenders, demonstrated by their relaxed state in taking a meal, implies that the events of 23 October 1055 were rather drawn out and, perhaps, that the 'burh' defences, notwithstanding their decayed condition, were sufficient to keep the enemy at bay for a while.

What is not in doubt is that Ralph knew about castles and French feudal warfare. Both the *Anglo Saxon Chronicle* and *Florence of Worcester* state that Ralph tried to make the English levies fight

have been Harold's work.[91] The 10th-century defences here were much decayed and would have provided little or no resistance to an enemy approaching the city from the west – the Whitecross area being where the battle is assumed to have taken place. As a result of the defeat, the city was pillaged; a great number of citizens were killed; the recently rebuilt cathedral was destroyed and several canons were also killed. Again, no mention was made of a castle or, indeed, of St. Guthlac's (Fig. 21).

The assumption that Earl Ralph built the first castle at Hereford seems to be based upon the on horseback in 1055 'against their custom' i.e. as knights, and this contributed to the disaster, although *Florence*, with justifiable patriotism, says that 'the earl with his Normans and Frenchmen set the example of flight' (Fig. 22). If Ralph was experimenting with knights, castles were an essential part of the same military system. Apart from his familiarity with castles in the Vexin, he was undoubtedly a close associate of Osbern Pentecost, the builder of Ewyas

Fig. 22.   Norman knights – victorious at Hastings (1066) but defeated at Hereford (1055).

Harold castle, not least because Ralph's son, Harold, eventually came into possession of the place, giving his name to it.[95] Bruce Coplestone-Crow, who explored the later history of Ewyas Harold, believed that Ralph must have built the castle at Hereford. He argues that the attack by Edric 'the wild' on Hereford castle in 1067, which is referred to in the *Anglo-Saxon Chronicle*, must have been the castle Ralph built as it was 'long before any Normans … appeared west of the Severn'.[96] However, this ignores the entry in the *Chronicle* immediately before the above which states that William I returned to Normandy in the spring of 1067 and left Bishop Odo of Bayeux and William fitzOsbern as regents who 'built castles far and wide throughout the land, oppressing the unhappy people'.[97] It would seem that Edric's attack upon Hereford was not pre-emptive, but was a response to the castle building activities of the Norman invaders.

Castle building was a very sensitive issue among the English. Swein Godwin son's revolt against Edward the Confessor in 1051 was in part a response to 'the foreigners who had built a castle in Herefordshire in Earl Swein's territory and inflicted all the injuries and insults they possibly could upon the King's men in that region'. This refers to Ewyas Harold and the 'injuries and insults' suggests that labour services were demanded from the English to build the earth and timber castles. With the decline in

'burh' building, which had called for impressive labour services, those demanded by Osbern would have been regarded as particularly irksome, especially when imposed by 'foreigners'. When Godwin and Harold, his son, returned from their exile in 1052 their first act of revenge was to 'outlaw all the Frenchmen who had promoted injustice and pronounced unjust judgements and counselled evil'. Osbern Pentecost appears to have been close to the top of their list and only escaped formal exile by fleeing to Scotland. Here he took up service with Macbeth, only to be killed soon after by Siward, the earl of Northumbria. Ralph, however, was spared exile being one of those intimates 'that the king was pleased to have about him, who were loyal to him and all his people'. Had Ralph been a castle builder, violating the precinct of St. Guthlac, even his privileged position as the king's nephew may not have been enough to save him.[98]

A recent study of Ralph suggests that he got on very well with Harold Godwinson who took over the earldom of Hereford after 1055. It has even been suggested that Harold may have been the godfather of his namesake, Harold, son of earl Ralph who became the lord of Ewyas Harold.[99] From the evidence that has been presented, it seems reasonable to argue that there was no castle at Hereford until William fitzOsbern arrived in 1067, having been given responsibility for Herefordshire by his absent king. Apart from any strategic considerations the main reason why he annexed the site of St. Guthlac's was simply because the precinct already contained a royal palace. Indeed, Ralph could well have been established in that palace in 1055 – in the corner of the town where the 'burh' defences seemed fairly intact. One small connection can be made directly with St. Guthlac's – his son, Harold, still held a tenancy from the minster at Whitney in west Herefordshire in 1066.[100]

The Norman Castle

The *Anglo Saxon Chronicle* makes the first reference to the castle at Hereford when describing the revolt of Edric 'the Wild' – the Shropshire thegn who reacted strongly to the castle-building activities of William fitz Osbern, King William's 'regent' in 1067. Although fitzOsbern received several grants of land in England, William would have regarded his presence upon the Welsh frontier as a priority as it remained very unstable and the conclusive nature of Harold's campaigns was not yet comprehended. A recent study of Norman settlement in Herefordshire suggests that fitzOsbern would have arrived early in 1067 and Edric's raid in August, accompanied by the Welsh, would have confirmed the urgency of the situation and stimulated castle building.[101] The destruction of the building excavated in 1999, which contained a loom (p. 24 and Pl. 2) may have occurred during this event. Attacking during the building process made good sense and, indeed, it was only two years previously that the Welsh had ruined Harold's aspirations to establish a foothold in Gwent by organising a pre-emptive attack upon his hunting lodge at Portskewet where many of his workmen were slain. According to the *Chronicle*, Edric and his allies also 'harried the county, reaching as far as the river Lugg [near Hereford?]'.[102] *Domesday Book* shows that fitzOsbern stepped directly into Harold's shoes in Herefordshire, not only in terms of possessions, but also finding Hereford, with its defences recently refurbished, valuable as a base. Since the *Chronicle* says Edric attacked 'the garrison of the castle' this may have taken place outside the city

and does not necessarily mean he attacked the castle itself. Fortunately, there were still Normans in Herefordshire who survived from Edward's reign and who were eager to ally with fitzOsbern and one of these, Richard fitzScrob of Richard's Castle, attacked Edric's possessions in the north of the county and south Shropshire, drawing him away from Hereford.[103]

Thus, fitzOsbern was provided with a window of opportunity to seize upon the defensive potential of the precinct of St. Guthlac where, it has been suggested, there may already have been some royal facilities. As the eastern side of the precinct was already defended by the 'burh' rampart, perhaps renewed by Harold, a simple ring-work, giving more definition to the enceinte, may initially have been all that was required. However, a large motte, which eventually supported a stone tower materialised in the 13th century and this is often attributed to fitzOsbern.[104] It may, however, have been built subsequent to fitzOsbern's time, after a sequence of developments which are paralleled elsewhere in England. Gloucester castle, also given impetus by fitzOsbern, is probably the closest and most thoroughly excavated example of an early medieval castle, which went through an extended process of development and may thus provide some useful lessons for Hereford.[105]

One of the most intriguing features of the surviving earthworks on Castle Green is Hogg's Mount, situated in its north-east corner. In the later Middle Ages it supported one of several round towers on the circuit wall of the developed castle. Even in its degraded state it remains a substantial earthwork which, encountered in the countryside, would be taken as a substantial motte. In the late 17th century it was measured by John Sylvester who computed it to be some 15m. in diameter at the top. It is something less today.[106] Looked at in conjunction with the pre-Conquest town plan it appears to occupy the site of the east gate of the Anglo-Saxon 'burh'. Such a position for an early castle has parallels at Winchester, Canterbury, Exeter and Gloucester where the reason for choosing these out-of-the-way sites appears to defer to the ecclesiastical

*Fig. 23. Hogg's Mount – possibly William fitz Osbern's motte, built
a respectful distance from the minster of St Guthlac,
and perhaps on the site of the royal hall (2006).*

have been given to the minster by the de Lacys as compensation, perhaps for the disturbance of its precinct in the early 11th century (Fig. 23).[108]

FitzOsbern's castle could have been given its first motte by his son Roger of Breteuil, but it was by no means complete when the castle was returned to royal hands in 1075 following Roger's rebellion. Now in the possession of the king, a major programme of reconstruction and reorganisation seems to have taken place, which led to the creation of the great western mound and the annexation of the whole of St. Guthlac's precinct. With Roger in prison and Walter de Lacy firmly in favour with the king, Hogg's Mount was apparently abandoned as the focus of the castle and recruited as a corner tower within the new enclosure. Like Lewes in Sussex and Lincoln, Hereford became one of those castles with two mottes. The spoil for the new motte presumably came from the deep excavations that were necessary for the development of the castle moats to the east and north, the latter finally dividing the religious precinct from the town and its market place (Fig. 24).

presence in the town as well as being strategic. There are no early examples of the name 'Hogg', but its origin perhaps comes from the Old English *ho(h)e* or Old Norse *haugr* – 'hill or mound', which would give it an early pedigree. It is likely that the precinct of St. Guthlac would have stretched down to the east gate, the very area where a royal hall might be anticipated. In 1067 fitzOsbern may have thrown up an earthwork enclosure next to the gate – as was the case at Gloucester, where the corner of the Roman enclosure was utilised. Again, following developments at Gloucester, a motte (Hogg's Mount) could have been added to the existing enclosure, exploiting the foundations of the east gate of the city to strengthen the mound, just as the Roman wall at Gloucester provided stability for the new motte there.[107] Indeed, the blocking of the gate may have been triggered by development of the Norman 'new town' which fitzOsbern inaugurated. As there was now a new east-west route through High Town, outside the earlier defences, the east gate beside St. Guthlac's was superfluous. It is interesting, in this regard, to notice that much of the garden ground between Hogg's Mount and the new church of St. Owen belonged to St. Guthlac in the Middle Ages and appears to

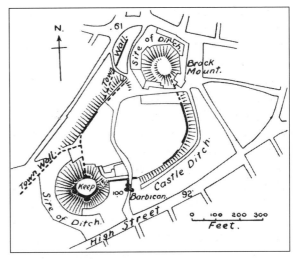

*Fig. 24. Lewes in Sussex – a castle, like
Hereford, with two mottes.*

Thus, on the basis of this rather imaginative reconstruction, Hogg's Mount may be fitzOsbern's contribution to Hereford castle. Although he was a mighty baron his English career was short – he died serving his king in Flanders in February 1071 – and his influence on the development of castles in the Welsh border has probably been exaggerated.[109] A recent study of the Great Tower at Chepstow castle has thrown doubt upon his role there, so it might be expected that he constructed something more modest at Hereford.[110] Surprisingly, *Domesday Book* is silent on the subject of Hereford Castle although it mentions seven other castles, many of which had direct connections with fitzOsbern. In other towns the building of a castle led to declining property values, which is commented upon in Domesday – for example at Warwick and Gloucester. In Hereford the number of dwellings owned by the bishop declined from 98 in the time of King Edward to 60 in 1086.[111] This is a large decline, out of all proportion to disturbance caused by castle building, and is much more likely to register the damage caused by the pillaging of Hereford in 1055 by the Welsh and their allies. If fitz Osbern's castle was a modest structure, either adjoining or on top of the redundant gate and perhaps on the site of the royal hall, there would have been no loss of burgages and little interference with St. Guthlac's.

The New Castle and the Spoilation of St. Guthlac's Precinct

The expansion of the castle appears to be tied up very closely with the fate of St. Guthlac's. Although many monasteries found their lands invaded by the Norman conquerors, St. Guthlac's problems, as has been shown, started much earlier in the reign of Cnut. The Norman barons in possession of the estates of St. Guthlac after 1066 simply stepped into the shoes of their English or Danish predecessors. In many respects the position of St. Guthlac's improved after the initial upheaval of the Conquest, especially under the patronage of the de Lacy family. After Roger's revolt, Walter de Lacy became the key

figure in the southern marches. From the Welsh perspective he had always been regarded as fitzOsbern's equal and certainly continued much of his work.[112] The completion of Hereford's 'new town' devolved into his hands. He founded two new churches dedicated to St. Peter and St. Owen at each end of the eastern arm of the 'new town' – the modern St. Owen Street.

St Peter's was provided with new endowments, some of which had previously belonged to St. Guthlac. Moreover, its dedication was St. Peter and St. Guthlac and its services were provided by the canons of the ancient minster. Although it is not stated explicitly in the sources, there is a clear impression that St. Peter's was created as a replacement for the church on Castle Green. The new church of St. Owen was also placed under the guardianship of St. Guthlac's as was the chapel of St. Martin, established within the bailey of the castle, which is first mentioned in 1154 by Hugh de Lacy as 'the chapel which my

Fig. 25. St Peter's church (David Cox c.1820) – built in 1085 in the middle of the Norman 'new town' and served by priests from St. Guthlac's in Castle Green.

ancestors founded'. It was presumably founded in the early 12th century. Clearly, the de Lacys were keen to breathe new life into the minster on Castle Green and in some respects were implicitly acknowledging its position as the mother church of Hereford (Fig. 25).[113]

After 1075 Hereford Castle was in the hands of the king but the foundation of St. Martin's suggests that the de Lacys were castellans and it is therefore likely that Walter, Roger or even Hugh supervised the extension of the castle. Roger was certainly a castle builder and erected one of the earliest stone keeps in the West Midlands at Ludlow in the 1090s.[114] The reorganisation of St. Guthlac's precinct with the building of a large motte between the minster and the cathedral may have commenced at this time. This would have made the position of St. Guthlac's and its graveyard increasingly untenable, hence the patronage of the de Lacys who may have appreciated the incongruity of the situation.

Moreover, as Hugh gave St. Peter's and St. Owen's to Gloucester Abbey in c.1101, he may already have suggested that the minster could secure itself by becoming a regular Benedictine priory, protected by Gloucester Abbey, a monastery very much in royal favour at this time.[115] Thus, the development of a more permanent fortress at Hereford might have been delayed until the 1080s or 1090s and was flagged-up by the de Lacy interest in St. Guthlac's. For some reason the community on Castle Green refused to budge. Maybe it was their deep-felt responsibilities for the ancient graveyard, their concern for the body and shrine of their patron saint and the sanctity of St. Ethelbert's Well. Whatever the reason, the minster remained in the midst of the hurly-burly that accompanied the building of Hereford castle.

It has been suggested above that the precinct of the minster, located at the south-eastern end of the Green may have remained

Fig. 26. Castle Green from the Cathedral tower –
well within range of Matilda's catapults in 1139 (1993).

outside the bailey of the new castle. However, the reality of life close to a military stronghold became very apparent during the civil war between Stephen and Matilda. It was in 1139 that the garrison of the castle, loyal to King Stephen, resisted an attack by Matilda's supporters, Geoffrey Talbot and Miles of Gloucester. The cathedral was occupied by their troops and a catapult was erected on its tower to bombard the castle. As the siege progressed, new earthworks, perhaps a counter-castle, were thrown up to attack the motte, the work being accompanied by the

> cries and lamentations of the townsfolk, because the earth of their kinsfolk's grave-yard was being heaped up to form a rampart and they could see, a cruel sight, the bodies of parents and relations, some half-rotten, some quite lately buried, pitilessly dragged from the depths.

Soon after this the garrison surrendered (Fig. 26).[116]

It seems likely that this graphic description tells the story of the final humiliation of St. Guthlac's minster. As the excavations on Castle Green confirm, the graveyard continued to receive burials during the early 12th century and, although it is possible, but not yet confirmed, that inhumations were taking place in the cathedral close, the magic of the holy-place, set aside from the city, continued to work, even though its position had been compromised since 1067 by the presence of the castle.[117] Nevertheless, the problems envisaged by the de Lacys of a religious site located in a place of war, now became all too evident. It seems likely that Matilda's forces broke into the eastern side of the castle bailey, perhaps using the old ford to cross the river. (During the Civil War in the 17th century this corner of the castle was again viewed as its Achilles heel). Pressing forward to the new motte, the attackers outflanked the minster and proceeded to dig up its graveyard to provide siege-works for the final assault upon the earthwork and timber castle.

As a result of this disaster, the saintly bishop of Hereford, Robert de Bethune, together with Roger fitzMiles (later earl of Hereford), intervened to save St. Guthlac's from further abuse and humiliation (Pl. 3). The *Gloucester Cartulary* states that in c.1143:

> Bishop Robert united the church of St. Peter of Hereford, situated in the market place, and the church of St. Guthlac, unsuitably situated within the circuit of the castle itself, and brought them together with all their private possessions and dignities to form one church, and by his authority as bishop consecrated it for the perpetual service of the Lord as the church of the apostles St. Peter, St. Paul and St. Guthlac, built by him from its foundations outside the city in a place most suitable for religion, in the time of Gilbert the abbot.

An earlier source suggests that the decision to surrender St. Guthlac's to the abbey of St. Peter's at Gloucester had been taken a little earlier by Miles of Gloucester who regarded himself as the heir to the de Lacy lordship in Herefordshire. In 1140 Matilda had made him earl of Hereford with a grant of the motte of Hereford and the whole castle.[118] In showing concern for St. Guthlac's, as the new castellan, he was fulfilling the programme inaugurated by his ancestors in c.1100. Thus the minster lost its independence and, on its new site in the Bye Street suburb (beneath the bus station and the modern hospital), it became a mere priory (Fig. 27). Its fate, in an oblique way, throws light upon its origins, for it followed in the footsteps of many other ancient 'clas' churches with British antecedents – like Llancarfan, Llanbadarn Fawr, Glasbury and Bromfield, near Ludlow – falling into the hands of Gloucester Abbey, which mopped-up many such establishments and became a veritable repository of 'celtic' traditions in the 12th century.[119] Remarkably, the priests of St. Guthlac's, soon to become Benedictine monks, failed to dismantle the wooden shrine of their patron saint, which remained within the bailey of the castle until it was accidentally destroyed in the reign of Edward I.[120]

Fig. 27.   The Priory in 1732 from Buck's North-East Prospect of the City of Hereford – *the site of the new St. Guthlac's converted into a residence after its dissolution in 1540.*

The Great Tower

The castle that Miles of Gloucester captured in 1139 was described as a *motam* or 'motte' – a vague term, which suggests that it was still an earthwork and timber structure. It is unlikely that Miles or his son Roger, who lost the castle to Henry II after his rebellion in 1155, would have re-built it. King Stephen had also granted 'the city, castle and whole county of Herefordshire' to Robert, earl of Leicester in 1141 but, notwithstanding his loyalty to Henry II, he was never allowed to enjoy it. The shire, the city and the castle remained in the hands of the king and when it appears in the *Pipe Rolls* in 1163, where expenditure is recorded amongst the expenses of the sheriff, the main feature on the motte is still referred to as the *domus* or 'house' – the living accommodation used by its lord or castellan.[121]

It is clear from the small sums spent on the castle, as recorded in the *Pipe Rolls* during the 1160s and '70s, that only minor work was taking place. They show, however, that there was a bridge (1165), gate (1174), and walls (1173) which were provided with *breteschiarum* – 'brattices' – wooden parapets or additional towers, added to the palisades.[122] 1173 was the year of a serious baronial revolt and the royal castles at Worcester and Gloucester were also put into a state of readiness. Henry was victorious at home and abroad and in 1176 he ordered his justices to ensure that the castles of his enemies were 'utterly demolished [and] razed to the ground'. Henry also entered into negotiations with the Welsh leaders, holding an important meeting at Gloucester in June 1175, followed by further negotiations that continued until May 1177. Perhaps, to provide an alternative venue for the necessary meetings, the 'king's house in Hereford castle' was put into repair in 1177. The work was extensive and cost £35 13s. 4d. – a not inconsiderable sum – and special attention was paid to the 'council chamber', which suggests a building in the bailey of the castle rather than on the motte. Indeed, this public building was presumably the successor to the Saxon hall and may have become the county or royal hall mentioned in 13th century documents. A further £33 was spent upon the 'king's house' in 1178-9 the work being inspected by Radulf of Grosmont.[123]

Although the *Pipe Rolls* indicate a growing interest in Hereford castle by the first Angevin king, there is little indication that Henry II made substantial additions in stone, albeit that a limekiln was referred to in 1181-2 and £1 6s. 6d. was spent on repairing a stretch of defective wall. In the same year John de Sanford was paid £4 for 'keeping the *mote* of Hereford'. Elsewhere in England, many timber towers, such as those at Shrewsbury and Clifford's Tower, York, survived in royal castles until the early 13th century.[124] In other cases, castles that appear to be important in *c.*1150 were never rebuilt in stone and were eventually abandoned. Hereford hardly impinged upon Richard I's consciousness, apart from when he sold the citizens a charter in 1189, which enabled them to enclose the town with a new bank and ditch and, ultimately, with gates and stone walls – a process that took well over a century.[125] Richard of Devizes recorded that the absence of Richard I on his crusade (1190-92) 'changed the face of the realm [and] certain nobles became busy; castles were strengthened; towns fortified, and moats were dug'. At Hereford Castle there was little activity, perhaps not surprisingly, as the same chronicler warned against establishing a *sedes* or 'seat' at Hereford because 'the Welsh are prodigal of the lives of others'. The *Pipe Rolls*, however, record that the sheriff was allowed £3 8s. in 1190-1 for work on the four gates of the city and the gate of the castle. Nothing was spent between 1192-3, but on Richard's return in 1194 work commenced on twelve brattices at the castle and repairs to the king's barn or *grangia* at Marden – a reminder of the earlier royal interest in this place.[126] In May 1194 Richard gathered his forces at Portsmouth and crossed the Channel to recover his continental possessions from Philip Augustus. He never set foot in England again (Fig. 28).

John (1199-1216) was much more hands-on as a king and modern historians believe that the revolt of the barons, which ultimately produced Magna Carta, was the result of too much efficient government by this hyperactive king. The barons preferred to be left to their own devices, as they had been under Richard.[127] John travelled the length and breadth of his kingdom and was regu-

larly found at Hereford. In the autumn of 1200, having signed a peace treaty with Philip Augustus, the king of France, and found a new wife, John made a tour of his English possessions and visited his castle in Hereford. He instructed the sheriff to make sure there was plenty of wine available and, following the visit, some minor repairs were carried out. Next year (1202) some serious work took place on the *turris* – 'tower', which cost £33 15s. 4d. A further £7 9s. 4d. was spent the following year on a 'small tower', accompanied by major work on the 'king's house', for which the sheriff claimed £68 9s. 4d.[128] The sudden appearance of the term *turris* deserves attention and suggests that the timber structures on the motte were being replaced with a stone tower or else this was a mural tower, perhaps built by his father.[129] Evidence from elsewhere in England suggest that £40 to £50 would pay for a shell keep – a stone wall replacing the wooden palisade on top of a motte. Close parallels are difficult to find, but in the late 13th century 50 perches of wall at Aberystwyth Castle cost only £37 10s., whilst a 50ft. tower at Harlech brought the master mason involved a sum of £11 7s. 6d. A stone tower, with internal floors and rooms, at a major castle in England was much more expensive, costing between £500 and £1000 in the early 13th century.[130] On the other hand, at Athelone in Ireland in 1211 Walter de Lacy, soon

Fig. 28. The domus on the motte at Hereford, referred to in the 12th century, would have looked much like the timber tower, surrounded by a palisade, depicted at Rennes on the Bayeux Tapestry.

Fig. 29. John's turris at Hereford may have been a simple shell keep, like that at Snodhill in west Herefordshire, built with straight sections of walling (1986).

to be the castellan of Hereford Castle, paid £129 12s. for a round tower, which is close to the global figure of £115 16s. laid out by John at Hereford between 1201 and 1203.[131]

Round towers were becoming particularly fashionable in the southern Marches around that time. John's loyal companion, William the Marshal, built the prototype at Pembroke in the 1190s and began another at Usk in John's reign. Similar towers were to appear at Longtown and Monmouth between *c.*1200 and 1220. The former was built by Walter de Lacy, the castellan of Hereford castle.[132] It would be surprising if John was not abreast of these developments, so possibly he was laying the foundations of his son's great tower at Hereford. On the other hand, the 'king's house' and its associated apartments

may still have survived in the bailey of the castle, where, it has been suggested, the Anglo-Saxon hall was located. Within a few years, however, the public activities within the castle were taking place in a 'shire hall' within the bailey, whilst some of the private apartments created by Henry III, John's son, were certainly located in the tower. The separation may have started in John's reign (Fig. 29).

One of the repeated criticisms of the chroniclers is that John eschewed the public life in the great hall and preferred the company of his young wife and a few intimates in the privacy of his *camera* or 'withdrawing room'.[133] Clearly, Hereford castle was becoming much more like a residential palace than a fortress, hence the increasing attention to two important appurtenances – 'the Hayes of Hereford' and the 'garden of the king'. As has been noted, the Old English kings were already using Hereford as a base for hunting, and among the 'customs of Herefordshire' listed in *Domesday Book* is the memorandum that: 'When the king was engaged in hunting, by custom one man from each house [in the city] went to stall game in the woodland'.[134] By the late 12th century the 'Hayes' had become the royal forest of Haywood with the castle at Kilpeck as its focus. John, however, still saw Hereford as an alternative base and, according to a later inquiry, 'unlawfully afforested the "vills" of Putson, Hinton and Hunderton, which belonged to the canons of Hereford'.[135] By extending the forest, John brought its boundaries down to the 'Southbridge' (Drybridge today) of Hereford (Fig. 30). Thus, the opportunities for haunting were brought within a bowshot of the castle and John took full advantage of this on his visits to Hereford in 1211, 1213 and 1214. These occasions were sweet for a king who loved 'haunting the woods and streams and greatly delighted in the pleasure of them', especially as the forest had been extended by a least 200 acres by the recovery of Treville Forest, to the north-west of Haywood, which Richard had granted to Dore Abbey in 1198. John, who was no friend of the Cistercians,

Fig. 30. David Cox, The Skirt of the Forest *(1855) – perhaps a memory of woodlands near Hereford where John hunted in the early 13th century* (Birmingham Art Gallery and Museum).

took possession of the Forest when he fell out with the pope. Thus, he was able to hunt from the Wye to the Dore without interruption and carry his game back either to Hereford or Kilpeck to feast in the sublime settings of these castles.[136]

One of the visual amenities of the castle – 'the king's garden' – was just below its ramparts, squeezed between the royal forest and the Wye. This first appears in the records in the early 12th century when it was in the possession of Hugh de Lacy. He gave a tithe of it to the church of St. Martin in the castle, which he had founded. The garden was said to be located across the Wye and the tithe was derived from the 'apples, hay and flax and everything else that grew there'.[137] At this date it was clearly a productive rather than an

ornamental garden and appears to be an ancient appurtenance of the castle or more likely the minster of St. Guthlac. It frequently returned to the hands of the king and in 1256 it was referred to as a 'herber' or flower garden. Nine years later the king granted it to Giles de Avenbury, treasurer of the cathedral, at a rent of 20s. *per annum*.

During a phase of repairs at the castle in the 1250s the garden was enclosed with 'the ditch of the king', which is noticed in 1422 and is known to us today as the Rowe Ditch. Archaeological evidence, however, suggests that the earthwork may originally have dated from the foundation of the garden in the 12th century. The garden was eventually restored to St. Guthlac's in return for services carried out by the religious community in

Fig. 31. The kyngisorchard *enclosed by Rowe Ditch – an important amenity for the royal castle (2006).*

the king's chapel within the castle. In a rental of the priory for 1456, the garden is said to extend to 10 acres and is described as the *Kyngisorchard*.[138] A similar garden existed at Gloucester castle in the 13th century. It was across the river Severn where it was reached by a bridge from the castle.[139] There is no record of a similar bridge at Hereford, so presumably it was not too inconvenient to use the Wye bridge in the city or the ford below the castle. Elsewhere, at Clun, Kenilworth

and Raglan, gardens like that at Hereford took on an ornamental character and, situated in full view of the castle, were developed as 'plesaunces' – a formal water garden with associated pavilions.[140] Apart from some low earthworks, little evidence for this exists at Hereford, but obviously there was something precious here, worth enclosing with a bank and ditch and protecting from the wild wood beyond (Fig. 31).

At the beginning of his reign John's relations with the Welsh princes were fairly good. The northern king, Llyewelyn the Great, was married to Joan, John's illegitimate daughter, and even supported John in his campaign against Scotland in 1209. In the south, William the Marshal and William de Briouze represented the king's interests. However, an abortive raid by John into Snowdonia in 1211 and the fall of de Briouze destabilised Wales and made it the primary problem for the young Henry III, John's eldest son. At first Henry relied upon baronial containment, but by the 1220s this was faltering and a royal presence in the southern Marches became essential. Thus, Henry had a pressing reason to complete his father's work in turning Hereford castle into a fortress palace and it received lavish expenditure, becoming one of the 'key points in the military geography of England'.[141]

Between 1239 and 1240 a new tower was built on the motte, reached by a stone staircase from the inner bailey.[142] The steps are indicated on Speed's drawing of the castle for his map of the city of 1610 (Fig. 32). This sketch, together with the description of John Leland early in the 16th century, brings us as close as we can expect to the Angevin castle.[143] The overall impression is of a modified shell keep with

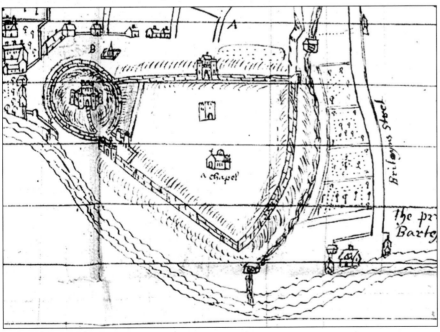

Fig. 32. A detail of Speed's plan of Hereford 1606, showing the great tower.

Fig. 33. Chateau Gaillard on the Seine. Richard I's masterpiece and a possible model for Henry III's great tower at Hereford (1982).

the outer wall of the tower being constructed either as a circular or flat-sided ring-wall, rather typical of the mid to late 12th century, but still being constructed in a modified form in the early 13th century. To this outer wall there has been added ten semicircular half-turrets – according to Leland – and in the centre there was a free-standing round tower. Although on a grander scale,the plan is similar to Tretower and Launceston and several other modified shell keeps where the round tower is regarded as a later intrusive addition. At Tretower and Launceston, however, the shell keep is attached to the tower, creating a subterranean passage around its base. At Hereford there appears to have been space for an open courtyard. The rebuilding of Launceston was carried out by Henry III's younger brother, Richard of Cornwall, but is said to be much later than Hereford and may have been influenced by

it rather than *vice versa*. The clustering of the turrets around the shell keep is reminiscent of the most famous castle of the age – Château Gaillard – where, being integral to the wall, they achieve a corrugated effect. Speed's sketch only shows five turrets, but even if we assume a fairly extended circumference for the wall, the ten noticed by Leland must have been fairly close together, achieving the same effect as Château Gaillard, which also has a square gate, like Hereford. Leland was impressed by the great tower, which he described as 'highe and very stronge', but he does not explicitly state that it was round. Speed's plan is also rather unhelpful, but in the early 13th century a square keep, in a land of round towers, would have been very regressive. As a round tower it would have been most impressive, and although it lacks the unique projections of the great tower at Château Gaillard, it would have dominated its surroundings in the same manner. John, it seems, never attempted to imitate Richard's masterpiece – he had unhappy memories of a failed attempt to relieve it in 1203, but his son carried no such baggage, and there may have been something of the 'Saucy Castle' – as Richard called Château Gaillard – in Henry's conception of the great tower at Hereford. Just as Richard's original threw out a challenge to the encroaching power of Philip Augustus, so the tower at Hereford may have been expected to intimidate Llywelyn the Great, who in fact died in the year of its completion (Fig. 33).[144]

In 1239-40 other towers around the bailey were either renewed or built for the first time. One, on the north side and presumably close to the gate, became the county gaol. The gate itself received attention, as did a small tower near the great tower, together with its passages. During the desilting of Castle Pool in 2006, probing at the south side of the pool revealed 'a solid feature' which, it has been suggested, may have been the remains of a bridge abutment (Fig. 34).

It lines up with the medieval road excavated in 1999 to the south of Castle House Hotel (p. 24).[145] Timber and stone for this work came from Haywood forest. The king's great chamber, presumably in the bailey, was panelled and whitened, ready to be coloured with diaper patterns. The roof was covered with wooden shingles. Nearby was the queen's chamber, but the assertive Eleanor was less happy with this and asked that it be lengthened by ten bays. Adjoining the royal apartments was a new private chapel, which the sheriff had been ordered to construct 'at the head of the oriole in the king's chamber' in 1233.[146] It was to be 'a decent chapel of the length of 25 feet'. This building was in addition to the free-standing de Lacy chapel of St. Martin built in the early 12th century. However, a later inquiry shows that the services in both were carried out by the monks of St. Guthlac's, who received an income of 100s. a year from various properties, including the 'king's garden' and the castle mill. The majority of this work was presumably

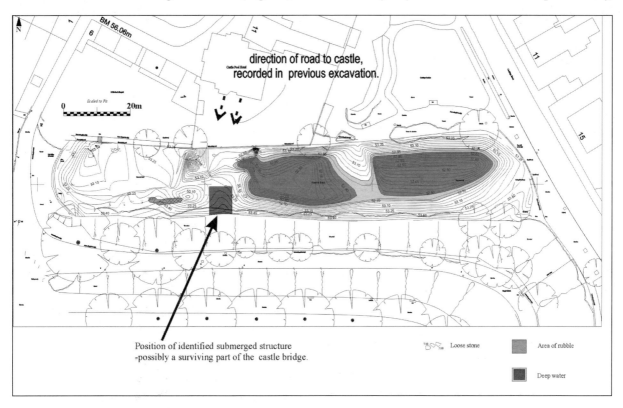

Fig. 34. Contour survey of Castle Pool Moat showing loose stone and areas of hard-packed rubble.

Fig. 35. The river cliff at Hereford continued to be a problem in the late 20th century and was reinforced with concrete slabs faced in stone in 1973.

completed before Henry met some of the Welsh leaders at Hereford in February 1241 – a sensitive moment, only a year after the death of Llywelyn the Great and with the kingship of North Wales disputed between his two sons.[147]

Work went on at the castle throughout Henry's reign. Much of it was designed to improve the comforts rather than reinforce its military potential. Repairs to the great gate and the bailey gate are referred to in 1251, when work was also required on 'the house in the great tower' – a phrase which hints at the secondary importance of the accommodation in the tower. The gravel banks, perhaps first thrown up to define the precinct of the minster and graveyard, provided poor foundations for the outer walls of the castle which were constantly in need of repair. In 1254 the sheriff was allowed £60 to build a stone quay on the riverside so as to prevent the castle wall from slipping into the Wye (Fig. 35).[148]

As new royal castles were built in Wales, Hereford became a centre of supply. Grain and salted meat were sent from the castle to Builth and Painscastle, and the 'quarrels' (iron bolts) of crossbows were stored here and distributed around the southern Marches. Occasionally 'engines of war' such as mangonels and trebuketts are mentioned, either being stored or repaired.[149] By the end of Henry III's reign a distinct impression is gained from the records that Hereford was no longer a front-line castle and as its other two roles – as a royal palace and a supply depot – also declined, it would become superfluous to need.

The Castle at War

The term of trial for Hereford castle came in 1264-5. To understand this, an excursion into the politics of the mid-13th century is necessary. Following the battle of Lewes in May 1264, fought to defend the novel concept of parliamentary government, Simon de Montfort captured King Henry and his son Edward and kept them as hostages. Simon then called a new parliament to discuss the affairs of the realm and expected the king and his supporters to accept the new arrangements, which were popular with the clergy and lesser folk of the kingdom. However, a group of marcher lords led by Roger Mortimer of Wigmore refused to accept the peace. Simon tried to negotiate with them using his ally, Llywelyn ap Gruffydd, to intimidate them. During the skirmishing that took place in the autumn of 1264, Roger and his supporters appeared before Hereford. The castle had already been handed over to Simon's friends and the citizens threw themselves enthusiastically into the defence of the city which, following a series of murage grants, was probably reasonably well fortified. Houses in the suburbs of the city were dismantled and burnt and the city ditch was widened and deepened. This meant that the mills employing the water in the ditch had to be destroyed – St. Guthlac's mill below the castle, the mill of Richard of Hereford, clerk, and another in St. Martin's, which perhaps used the water running along the Rowe Ditch. When Roger and 'the great men' arrived with banners displayed, they 'grievously assaulted the town', plundering St. Guthlac's priory in Bye Street, the leper hospital of St. Giles, probably in St. Owen Street, and the 'house of Aylmeston [now Aylestone Court Hotel], to the damage of the bishop and chapter'. Finally, they 'cast fire upon Bishop's Street [Commercial Street]' before retreating to the north of the county where Llywelyn had created a diversion by attacking Roger's castles (Pl. 4).[150]

Mortimer and his allies made a temporary peace with Simon at Worcester. Parliament reassembled in March 1265 and another attempt was made to establish a permanent settlement. But many nobles, including Roger, refused to collaborate and in May Simon moved with his royal hostages first to Gloucester and then to Hereford, where he hoped to deal with Roger and the marcher loyalists. Meanwhile, supporters of the king were returning from exile and all that was required to re-ignite the royalist cause was an energetic leader – a role played enthusiastically by Henry's son, Edward. Simon realised his fortunes were declining and the prince was kept under close guard in Hereford castle by Henry de Montfort, one of Simon's sons. He slept in Edward's chamber, but shared his duties with Thomas of Clare, the brother of Gilbert, the earl of Gloucester, hitherto one of Simon's staunchest supporters. On 28 May, just after Whitsunday, the prince, accompanied by Thomas of Clare, took exercise on Widemarsh and made a dash for Wigmore castle (Fig. 36). The king's supporters were galvanised into action, the Severn fords were guarded and Edward recovered the royal castle at Gloucester. Simon could see himself becoming trapped on the Welsh border and having secured Llywelyn's moral and financial support, but only a few Welsh troops, he crossed the Severn at Kempsey below Worcester, eluding Edward who had returned to the Midlands to intercept Simon's eldest son, Henry, at Kenilworth. The younger Simon was bringing an army from the south to aid his father. On 3 August Simon reached Evesham and was defeated by Edward and Roger Mortimer on the following day. Simon and his knights fought to the last in a circle around the feeble king, who was rescued alive in the final *mêlée*. Earl Simon's head was struck off and sent to the wife of Roger Mortimer, but he was buried at Evesham in a grave that is still well marked – 'his legend grew, his miracles were told among the people and collected'.[151]

The castle and city of Hereford had stood firm against the assault of Roger Mortimer and, as far as one can tell, this was the last time until the 17th-century Civil War that anyone – king, baron or peasant – lifted a finger in anger against either. Three months after Evesham the provisional government established a commission of three barons to enquire into the 'robberies and other trespasses committed in the city and suburbs of Hereford by Sir Roger de Mortuo Mari'. As a result of their inquiry the citizens were granted £100 'for their expenses in the amendment and defence of the town'. The commissioners were also asked to view the defects of the castle, which resulted in a long list of instructions to the sheriff who was required to:

> fit the tower with joists and roof it with lead, make a bridge to the tower, repair the king and queen's halls, chambers, kitchens, the larder, the knights' chamber, the king's chapel, the stable and two turrets; finish a chamber lately begun for the king's clerks, make a bake house, repair the walls descending from the tower to the city and Wye; repair the king's hall belonging to the

Fig. 36. The remains of Widemarsh Moor, flooded in 1979, where Prince Edward took exercise and escaped from Hereford castle in May 1265.

almonry, the halls where the county courts are wont to be held, the Exchequer chamber in the inner bailey; to make a building for housing engines, the gate beneath the tower, the swing bridges there and prison within the castle with all necessary repairs.[152]

This must represent the best description of the castle at its zenith, but there is little evidence to indicate that the comprehensive refurbishment planned here ever took place. Ironically, the sheriff was Roger Mortimer who in 1269 found himself very much out of pocket, claiming £445 10s. 3d. for 'munitions at Hereford castle including the wages for serjeants and knights dwelling within the garrison at Hereford castle during the disturbances of the realm'. Apart from the citizens, only the prior of St. Guthlac's seems to have received adequate compensation. In 1266 he was allowed to 'raise again a mill below the castle of Hereford' and provided with sixteen

oaks from Haywood Forest to repair the priory in Bye Street.[153]

Edward went on to punish de Montfort's ally, Llywelyn, and subdued Wales between 1277-82. Many new castles were built in north Wales, which helped to bankrupt the crown. Scotland was next on Edward's agenda and although there were occasional surveys of the fabric, Hereford castle slipped from purview of the government. In 1281, for reasons unknown, the sheriff allowed the military stores in the castle to be destroyed by fire. Perhaps they were old and redundant – like the castle.[154]

Late Medieval Decline

Hereford castle achieved its apogee in the reign of Henry III (1216-72) with the building of the great tower in 1240. Thereafter, for the remainder of the 13th century, there were regular surveys followed by minor repairs, but nothing substantial was added to the Angevin castle.[155] In 1316 Edward II instructed a commission to view the defects of the castle, but when his wife, Queen Isabella, arrived in Hereford in 1326, she was persuaded to take lodgings at the bishop's palace. The security was poor and she lost four bags of account rolls and inquisitions, carried off from her chamber by three knights.[156] The weakness of the castle was also apparent in 1344 when the justices conveyed certain felons to the castle for hanging, but a 'multitude of people' laid siege to it, broke in and carried off the prisoners.[157] The gaol was an important facility for the county as well as the kingdom and it appears to have been rebuilt at the expense of the county community in 1291.[158] References to gaol delivery to Hereford castle continue throughout the Middle Ages and in the 17th century it was still said to be within the gatehouse overlooking the castle pool.[159]

The castle continued to be inhabited by a keeper and porter, but references to their appointment become intermittent as the Middle Ages progress. The saviour of the castle should have been John of Gaunt (1340-99) who in c.1390 became its governor and began to assemble building materials, intending to make the castle his 'chief abode'. Unfortunately, Richard II, suspicious of his over mighty uncle, restored royal custody. As a result, Gaunt turned his attention to Kenilworth, where his apartments, including a magnificent great hall, are regarded as one of the climaxes of domestic architecture in the Middle Ages.[160] Back under royal control Hereford castle continued to decay.

Among the facilities provided within the castle by Henry III for the use of the local community was a county hall. This provided a courtroom for the activities of the sheriff and the itinerant justices. As late as 1381 rent from the royal estates in the county was being paid to the sheriff in 'the king's castle at Hereford', but soon after this the county hall became untenable and in 1393 Richard II granted a licence to the citizens to acquire a messuage valued at 60s. as 'they have no house within the castle and the city to hold their sessions and assizes'.[161] The Booth

Hall in High Town, which came into existence at this time, presumably provided a venue for these occasions.

The declining state of the castle is epitomised by the regular grants of herbage within the 'king's castle and the king's orchard', which occur from the late 14th century.[162] In effect sheep and cattle were being used to keep down the vegetation, a procedure that was to continue until the early years of the 20th century. (Fig. 37) A grant of herbage within a royal castle in the later Middle Ages appears to have been regarded as a privilege. For example in 1427, Henry VI made a grant to Thomas Petit as a reward for his part in the capture of the rebel, Sir John Mortimer, three years earlier. No doubt, Petit's herbage rights made him feel 'king of the castle'.[163]

Although the castle slumbered during this period, the crown was not inactive in defending its proprietary rights. Sharpened, perhaps by John of Gaunt's aspirations for the castle, Richard II glanced occasionally in this direction. In 1396 he reminded the prior of St. Guthlac's that, according to letters patent issued by Henry III, the convent was to celebrate divine service in the king's chapel within the keep of the castle three times a week. St. Guthlac's enjoyed property granted to it by the king, in return for this service, worth 100s. a year. This included the Castle Mill but 'for the last twenty years or more' the prior had ceased to maintain a chaplain and the king's interest was 'grievously damaged'.[164] Richard was also sensitive about encroachments upon the entrance to the castle. In front of the great bridge, on a site occupied today by St. Ethelbert's almshouses and the Castle Hotel, there was clearly an open space – large enough it seems for a market place. In 1395 a commission was established to inquire into the buildings erected by the tenants of the Dean and Chapter, which prevented access to the land adjoining the fosse and bridge of the castle 'where the corn market has long been held'.[165] Richard's interest in Hereford castle suggests that in different circumstances, the crown may have restored it as a royal centre.

Fig. 37. Sheep grazing on Castle Green in 1909.

Significantly, it was one of the royal castles ordered by Henry IV to be refortified during the Glyn Dwr rising. Unlike many in the list, work actually seems to have taken place. The roof of the great tower was repaired, corner towers were refurbished and, where the riverside wall had collapsed, oak paling was erected. In all £100 was spent.[166] This was the last time before the Civil War that the military potential of Hereford castle was taken seriously.

The 15th-century records of the Dean and Chapter indicate that the Lancastrian and Yorkist kings had few misgivings about granting away the appurtenances of the castle for small rents. In 1438 they granted away a garden in Castle Street, which extended on the east as far as the castle bridge and on the south to the castle ditch. In *c.*1580 this plot provided a new site for the hospital of St. Ethelbert, hitherto sited in Broad Street.[167] Further west, an area of the castle ditch 'from the place where the bridge of the said castle was of old, to the stone wall at the end of the ditch

on the east' was granted in 1472 to John Welford. Today, this appears to be part of the site occupied by the Castle Hotel and it is interesting to notice that the castle bridge, said by John Leland to be 'clean down' in *c.*1540 had disappeared long before 1472 (Fig. 38).[168]

Another area where the crown seemed willing to compromise on the strength of the castle was the barbican – an apron of land below the keep, close to the cathedral precinct, which in the High Middle Ages provided a defensive outwork for the keep beyond the moat. Henry VI granted 'the waste called the barbigan' to a clerk called John Grene in 1453. It was said to encompass a piece of land 7 perches (*c.*112ft.) between the castle and the Dean and Chapter land and 3 perches and 2ft. from the river Wye (*c.*50ft.). By 1497 the barbican seems to have been in the hands of the 'mayor and citizens of Hereford' and is referred to in the boundary clauses of a grant by the Dean and Chapter to the custos of St. Ethelbert's Hospital. It remains in the hands of the City Council today.[169]

Fig. 38. The bridge giving access to the castle crossed the pool close to the Castle House Hotel on the right.

The Tudor Years

John Leland's description of the castle in *c*.1540 is very well known and only a few comments are required here.[170] He confirmed that the 'great bridge of stone archis' was already in ruins, and that the water, which enclosed both the 'dungeon' (great tower) and the two 'wardes', no longer flowed through the castle, although it powered a mill 'within the castle' – perhaps on the site of the mansion called The Fosse. More pertinently, for the future use of the castle, he noticed that the 'dungeon' was in relatively good condition – 'high and very stronge, havynge on the upper waull or warde 10. towers *forma semicirculari*' – and one great tower in the inner ward. There was also a 'faire chepelle' with a circular apse standing in Castle Green – probably the 12th century chapel of St. Martin, and not St. Cuthbert (St. Guthlac) as

Leland believed. There was a 'plentiful spring' within the castle, which on a later journey to Wales, in the late 1530s, he confirmed was St. Ethelbert's well. In the same postscript he referred to bones found in the river-bank 'not gigantic but certainly of unusual size'. These, of course, came from the burial ground associated with the church of St. Guthlac. Finally, he stated, with a certain amount of exaggeration, that Hereford castle 'be of as great a circuite as Windesore'.[171]

At the time that Leland was recording the antiquities of England on his itinerary, the president of the Council in the Marches of Wales, Rowland Lee, Bishop of Coventry, was making a survey of Wigmore castle and considering its restoration. Did he also cast an eye towards Hereford, as a potential southern base for the Council? Gaol delivery still continued, although

Leland makes no mention of the gatehouse, which was still sufficiently intact to receive prisoners. In 1513, for example, the gaol was full of recruits who had fled from the royal army on its way to France with the king (Henry VIII) who was convinced he was Henry V. In 1536 the unfortunate Thomas ap Hugyn was incarcerated there for expressing his sympathy for the 'rebels in the North' – the Pilgrims of Grace.[172] Within the castle there was another local amenity – the King's Pound'. By 1521 the citizens of Hereford were no longer using this amenity, perhaps because of problems of access. Consequently, the bishop's steward was putting stray animals in his pinfold and charging 5d. for retrieval.[173]

The vegetation within the circuit of the castle walls continued to flourish, prompting the crown, rather irregularly, to renew the lease for herbage. In 1569 it was granted to George Tirell, a gentleman usher of Queen Elizabeth, whose family in the 14th century was fairly prominent in the county.[174] That a courtier should be interested in grazing the castle pasture is surprising and there is a suggestion here that the lease of a royal castle, however ruinous, conveyed some sort of prestige, especially for a family with ancient roots in the county.

CHAPTER IV

Royalty : The Civil War

Whereas castles had been virtually ignored as defensive structures during the Wars of the Roses, the English Civil War saw a revival of interest in medieval fortifications, albeit enhanced with new earthen defences for artillery. It is perhaps ironical that the time of trial for Hereford castle arrived in 1643 at a point when its symbolic significance, hinted at earlier in the grants of herbage, was about to be realised. In different circumstances, the remains of the castle may have been preserved in private hands as an ancient monument or refurbished as a gothic mansion.

By the early 17th century, antiquarianism, which had its roots in the Renaissance, began to have beneficial results for the remains of England's medieval past. A number of 'new' castles were built in this era including Ruperra (Glamorgan), Lulworth (Dorset) and, it seems, Croft in Herefordshire.[175] At the same time there was increasing pressure upon the Stuart kings to sell or lease redundant royal castles. With royal finances in crisis and parliament reluctant to grant new subsidies, the crown was only too willing to satisfy this demand. Thus, in 1626, Robert Terswill, the Surveyor General of the Royal Woods, was instructed to view the ruinous castles at Gloucester and Hereford to see if they could be put to any profitable use. Four years later, Hereford was granted to Sir Gilbert North, a minor courtier and brother of the colonial promoter, Roger North (1585-1652). Within two

months he had conveyed it to William Page of London who held it by feudal tenure from the manor of East Greenwich. It remained in the possession of his family until 1646.[176] This transaction, reminiscent of the speculation associated with the distribution of monastic property a century earlier, suggests that North acted as a go-between for Page, whose motive in purchasing a remote royal castle remains a mystery. As there is little indication that he sold any of the fabric for building materials, it was most likely that, like the sale of modern castle sites and lordships, its possession conveyed status.

Page found the two acres of the castle tenanted by John Mason, who enjoyed rights of herbage and fishing along the river bank from the canonical house of John Green, clerk, to the Hereford Mills. The rights also included the area of the barbican. In total, Mason paid a rent of 20s. per annum.[177] Nowhere in the document is there any suggestion that the castle was habitable. Indeed, the terminology of the grant with its long list of features – yards, ditches, trenches, fosses, pools, quarries etc – suggests a lack of specific knowledge of the site by the clerk who produced the document.

John Webb, author of the *Memoirs of the Civil War in Herefordshire* – one of the best 19th-century local histories of the conflict – assures us that 'No mention is made of the castle in any account of the military operations' close to

Fig. 39. Buck's north-east prospect of Hereford (1732) – showing the castle mount (8) clearly elevated above the adjoining buildings of the city.

Hereford.[178] Nevertheless, the castle was noticed and refurbished by the parliamentarians, becoming a symbol of their unwelcome presence in a royalist county. In fact, the gaol was still being used right up to the eve of the Civil War, for in 1640 the sheriff of the county, Thomas Alderne, found himself imprisoned by Charles I in the 'gatehouse' for not collecting ship money.[179] Apart from this, the royalists seemed to have virtually ignored the castle. When Sir Richard Cave, the royalist governor of Hereford, received news of the approach of a parliamentary force under the command of Sir William Waller on 25 May 1643, he went at first light to the castle 'being the best place to make discovery' of the enemy and found Waller less than a mile from the city. It must be assumed that, to gain this intelligence, he must have climbed the great tower (Fig. 39). Later, during his court martial, he stated that he also noticed that the city could be entered from the ford beneath the castle and suggested 'a breastwork should be cast-up to defend the entrance to the castle by the mill'. His advice was ignored.[180]

During the Scottish siege of July and August 1645, the new royalist commander. Barnabus Scudamore, described for Lord Digby the 'sallies made by us at the castle to good effect', but does not suggest that the castle was in any sense re-fortified.[181] When the king visited the city in

Fig. 40. Clifford's Tower at York – similar to the tower on the motte at Hereford before it was refurbished by Colonel Birch.

of the 'speedy fortifying' of the castle, which by the beginning of March 1646 was 'so strengthened that with the help thereof of 460 men kept that city'.[185] A later parliamentary survey mentions that Birch covered the tower of the keep with lead taken from the Chapter House, whilst Webb adds that stone was robbed from the house of the royalist Sir Samuel Aubrey at Clehonger, who had recently died. Timber, also presumably extracted from the estates of local royalists, was delivered to the castle in May 1646, and in August Birch legalised his occupation of the castle by obtaining a conveyance from Edward Page.[186] Albeit the castle was repaired and garrisoned, it seems that

September of the same year, he was accompanied by Sir Henry Slingsby who remarked that the castle resembled that at York 'for it hath a round tower mount'd upon a hill; like Clifford Tower, and ye mills near it, with some little works about' (Fig. 40).[182]

The 'little works' could have been thrown up by Scudamore who, in his *Defence* (1645) refers to the 'sally ports of the castle', the keys for which had been misappropriated, causing Scudamore to suggest that they had been used by informers who carried intelligence to the parliamentary commander, Colonel Birch.[183] More likely Slingsby is referring to the remains of the medieval walls and ramparts. When excavations took place close to Nelson's column in the 19th century, military weapons 'such as used at the time of the parliamentary wars' were discovered.[184]

Colonel Birch's Reconstruction

In December 1645 Colonel John Birch finally secured Hereford for parliament. He found the citizens confused and demoralised by several years of martial law, but nevertheless still showing 'partiality for the cavaliers and papists' (Fig. 41). Being unwelcome, the garrison needed protection, and Birch's secretary Roe wrote later

Fig. 41. The monument to Colonel Birch in Weobley church – dressed as a military dictator?

Fig. 42. Sir Robert Harley – purchaser of the castle from Colonel Birch in April 1647.

Birch lived in the bishop's palace, which he later leased to the parliamentary sequestration officer, Silas Taylor.[187]

Following a widespread revolt in March 1647 by the unpaid parliamentary army and fanned by extremist groups like the Levellers, parliament proposed that Hereford should be 'disgarrisoned' and that Birch's regiment should be sent to Ireland. Significantly, the 'new works' at the castle were to be demolished, although the castle itself – presumably the great tower – was to be manned by Colonel Samuel Moore with a reduced detachment of 160 men.[188] Dislodging Birch's men was far from easy and within their 'new works' they were a threat to both parliament and the local community. Birch initially supported his men, but by March 1647 he was M.P. for Leominster and realised that his military career was at an end. In April 1647 he sold the castle to Sir Robert Harley, the leading figure on the Parliamentary Committee for Herefordshire, for £600 (Fig. 42). Harley and his fellow committee members, basically the moderate and middling gentry of the county, hoped this would be the first step in getting rid of the troublesome garrison. The soldiers, however, who had still not been paid, mutinied and when Birch came to Hereford in July to mediate, they seized him and his brother, plus the £200 they had found within his coffer in the tower. He was eventually released and the House of Commons voted £7,500 to pay the arrears demanded by the soldiers, whereupon they disbanded and went home.[189]

Sir Robert's conveyance describes the castle in the same terms as the grant made to Sir Gilbert North in 1630, but an endorsement states that the purchasers, which included five other members of the Parliamentary Committee for Herefordshire – Edward Harley (Sir Robert's son), Walter Kyrle, Bennett Hoskins, Edmund Weaver and William Crowther – would eventually 'employ the castle and lands ... for the public use, benefit and advantage of the county of Hereford and the inhabitants thereof'. Sir Robert had apparently provided the £600 purchase money and was expecting to be reimbursed, but in a memorandum drawn up by his son Edward in 1668, because of the great sums necessary to disband Birch's regiment, this had never been done. As the principals in the transaction passed away, the truth of the situation became more difficult to ascertain. In 1682, Sir William Gregory, Baron of the Exchequer and a native of the county, wrote to Sir Edward Harley indicating that he was under the impression that the 'county raised the money that paid for the castle' and that Sir Robert Harley was simply chief among the trustees. Thus, the title to the castle remained in doubt throughout the late 17th and early 18th centuries. Gradually, the county magistrates, often with the tacit encouragement of the Harley family, assumed *de facto* control but, understandably, felt insecure about the legal status of the conveyances and tenancies they began to issue for the castle and its appurtenances. Eventually, in 1748 after much serious but generally friendly, lobbying and petitioning, Edward Harley, earl of Oxford, discharged the county magistrates of their debt to his family, which with interest was calculated at £5,160.[190]

The Parliamentary Surveys

As has been mentioned, late in 1647 Birch and his garrison had been removed, but the castle, with the consent of the Parliamentary Committee, remained in the hands of the new governor and his troop. Colonel Moore was replaced by Major Wroth Rogers as governor of Hereford sometime early in 1648. He faced a crisis, having discovered that the seizure of Hereford castle was one of the objectives of the royalist rebellion led by Sir Henry Lingen in July 1648. He was obliged to spend £200 'victualling and repairing the castle' for which he was subsequently reimbursed. The rebellion was nipped in the bud by the arrest of several suspected royalists, but the Council of State was determined to maintain a garrison in the castle as few people in Hereford were 'well affected to the present government [and] might well declare against the commonwealth and give a beginning to new troubles'.[191] When Silas Taylor, the sequestration officer for the county, a cultivated man and friend of Samuel Pepys, arranged for a music meeting at the Bishop's Palace in January 1652 and invited the royalist gentry, the garrison of the castle, sensing a 'papist plot', were 'kept to their arms'.[192]

On 14 December 1652 parliament had the castle surveyed, providing the first detailed view of its condition since Leland's visit over a century before.[193] The 'tower on the mount' was noticed, which together with the lead from the Chapter House was worth £40 as building materials. Below it there was a dwelling house called the Governor's Lodge – presumably the present Castle Cliffe House – which had three rooms above ground and three below. There were two buildings on Castle Green; one was probably the 12th century church of St. Martin, which had

been used by the guard and for quartering soldiers. The Green was enclosed by the ruins of an old wall 'with diverse fortifications built upon it' – perhaps the ramparts erected by the parliamentary garrison. On the north wall there was the 'old ruinous gatehouse' also covered with lead from the Chapter House. This was worth £25 and the gross value of the site came to £85. It would seem that Birch may have held the county community to ransom by selling Castle Green to their representatives for £600, but the value of the materials alone does not necessarily equate with the value of the site as a whole.

The same surveyors moved across to the barbican, where on the east side they noticed a public washing place, close to St. Ethelbert's Hospital, which had been rendered inaccessible by the master of the hospital who had railed off the connecting thoroughfare – presumably the passage that exists today. Major Rogers, now promoted to Lieutenant Colonel, was ensconced in the College of the Vicars' Choral and owned an orchard forming the western boundary of the barbican. The surveyor noted that there had been a house in the barbican, standing near the castle, which had been 'pulled down in the time of the wars'. Adjoining it there had been a garden and a bowling alley 'all ruined at the same time'. A petition to the mayor's court in 1664, indicates that it belonged to a brickmaker, Henry Traunter, who claimed he had a grant from Charles I in 1645, when on his visit to the city after the battle of Naseby, 'to build a cottage on the waste of the castle'. It had subsequently been demolished by Wroth Rogers, who had carried the building materials away to repair the College.[194] The surveyors were puzzled by the claim that one Bryant Newton had a lease granted by the city of Hereford for the 40 perches that made up the barbican, although neither the city nor Newton could provide evidence of their claims to the property. The surveyors assumed that in 'the time of Charles Stuart' it owed rent to the crown.

In 1654 the Lord Protector, Oliver Cromwell, was seeking means to reduce expenditure, following the First Dutch War. He consulted

Colonel Birch on the removal of certain garrisons. Hereford was considered, but Birch advised that as the place stood between north and south Wales it should be maintained, adding that 'the countries and people there were not so well affected as he could wish'. Other voices clearly advised that Hereford should be disgarrisoned and in April 1655 the Council of State ordered the demolition of the castle to make 'Col. Birch's house untenable' – presumably the great tower.

The moat was to be filled up and breaches were to be made to allow free passage into the castle. Colonel Rogers was ordered to do the work within two months.[195] In fact, the castle and its garrison, commanded by Rogers, remained inviolate until 1660.

CHAPTER V

Recreation : The Development of the Park

The Restoration: Demolition and 'Public Use'
The order to demolish the great tower was presumably made by the Second Protectorate Parliament or the 'Rump', restored to power in May 1659. The work took place in April 1660 – a month before Charles II re-entered London – and was carried out by a team of *c.*30 masons and labourers, receiving, on average, 1s. per day (Fig. 43). Two months earlier Captain Green's company of foot in Hereford, numbering about 90 soldiers, had been paid off and so the Civil War ended for Hereford.[196]

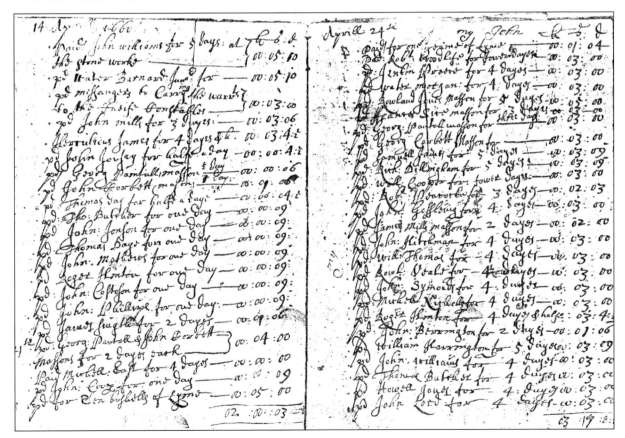

Fig. 43. The accounts for the demolition of the great tower in April 1660.

Sir Edward Harley's memorandum of 1668 indicates that, following the demolition of the great tower, the county magistrates acted quickly to exploit their newly acquired asset. Castle House on the Green (Castle Cliffe) was leased to Robert Stallard for £10 *per annum* and the gatehouse to Mary Bosworth for 2s. 6d. The stone, presumably from the demolished tower, was to be employed by the magistrates to build a workhouse or house of correction. Stallard, meanwhile (1662), tried to sub-let the Castle House to Sir William Sandys, who had been appointed by Act of Parliament to make the Wye navigable. But no agreement could be reached and so the magistrates recovered the lease and instead used Castle House as the house of correction. The stone from the tower was sold to the Dean and Chapter to build a dining hall for the Vicars' Choral, and the city bought the rest to erect a tolsey at the east end of High Town. Gravel was also sold from the site of the tower for road making and in 1674 two justices, Bridstock Harford and Herbert Aubrey, were instructed to take a view of the castle and 'pluck down' any timber or other materials which were 'in danger

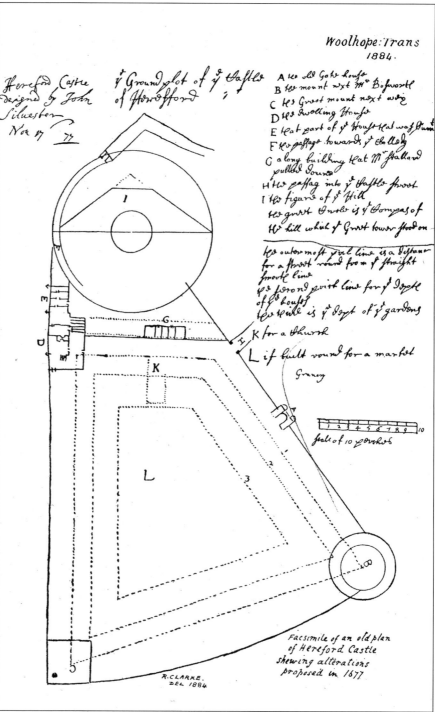

Fig. 44. *John Silvester's plan of Hereford castle, 17 November 1677.*

of falling'. Early in the 1670s the gatehouse was regained from Mary Bosworth and was then repaired for storing the county records.

Plate 1 (above).
Parch marks on Castle Green,
Summer 2006.
St. Guthlac's is to the left of
the Bowling Green, whilst
St. Martin's, on the site of
an earlier timber church, is
shown as a rectangle left of
centre. (Derek Foxton
Collection).

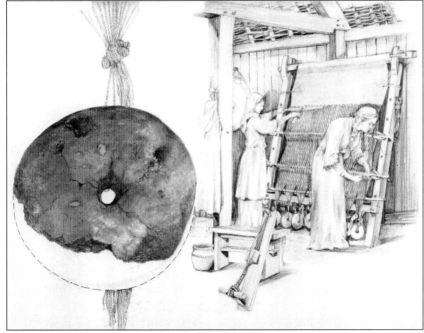

Plate 2 (left).
An artist's impression of an
upright loom and loom-weight
as found in the Castle House
excavations. (Archaeological
Investigations Ltd.).

Plate 3. The proximity of the royal castle denied Hereford this impressive ruin.
Croyland Abbey, a watercolour by John Sell Cotman c.1804, at the site of St. Guthlac's hermitage
in Lincolnshire. (Copyright: Trustees of the British Museum).

Plate 4. A reconstruction of the castle as it would have appeared during the crisis of 1264.
The author would favour a round great tower, rather than a square one, whilst the ten turrets
on the ring wall need to be closer . (Dr. and Mrs. Heijn).

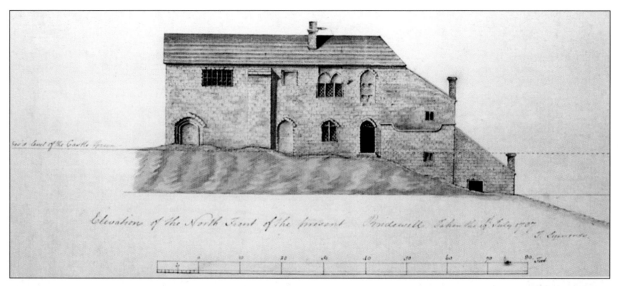

Plate 5 (top). Thomas Symonds' elevation of the north front of the existing Bridewell, 19th July 1787.
Plate 6 (centre). His elevation of the north front of the proposed Bridewell, c.1788 .

Plate 7 (left). Looking downstream to the new gardens and the riverside walk with the ferryman's cottage on the far left, c.1905.

Plate 8. The Victoria Suspension Bridge.

Plate 9. Nelson's column with formal bedding, close to the recently enclosed bowling green, c.*1920.*
(Derek Foxton Collection).

Plate 10. A postcard view looking eastwards along the Upper and Lower Walks, c.1900.

Plate 11. The Wye from Castle Green, c.1910.

Plate 12. The riverside 'alcove' at the northern end of the suspension bridge, c.1918.

Plate 13. The Green in the 1920s.

Plate 14. Castle Green and Bishop's Meadow in the early 20th century.

Plate 15. The Cantilupe Gardens in the 1930s with the green keeper's punt and the (?)royal swans.

ELEVATION

ELEVATION

Plates 16 & 17. Alternative designs for the bowling green clubhouse, 1932.

However, she retained a lease for a:

parcel of ground, moat, ditch on the north side of the green of the castle extending from the town wall of Hereford at the east unto the stonewall now erected for a head or dam to keep in the water in the said part of the said ditch or moat at the west … in breadth from the foundation of the wall on the top of the bank of the castle green to the garden of Mary Bosworth and other small gardens or parcels of ground adjoining thereto.

Subsequently, this property was vested in Thomas Carpenter Esq. and Robert Dobyns, whilst the pasture of the Green was rented for 30s. by John Pill Esq. Richard Stallard was still on the scene in 1670 when the justices demolished the small house he had built on the north-west side of the Green. It is marked on John Silvester's plan of 1677 as 'G – the long building that Mr. Stallard pulled down' (Fig. 44).[197]

When the city authorities heard that Sir William Sandys was proposing to establish a quay at the castle, they drew up a memorandum expressing their concern about 'the erecting of shops and exposing for sale all sorts of goods within the confines of the castle to the prejudice of the city'. Perhaps to kill the enterprise they prohibited the carriage of coal from the castle in 'iron bound waynes'. In the event, Sandys' scheme for the Wye navigation was never fully realised and the creation of a burgeoning entrepot at the castle was deferred.[198] However, in 1677 John Silvester, a carpenter/joiner, who appears to have served his apprenticeship in London and came to Hereford to participate in the repair of the cathedral after the Restoration, becoming sexton in 1669, drew up some remarkable proposals for the castle.[199] In the centre of the Green, a surviving building, perhaps St. Martin's chapel, was to be 'built round as a market granary' – presumably a market hall. Around it were terraces of houses, much like an Italian piazza with gardens at the rear. Had this been constructed it would have been the first piece of regular town planning outside the City of London. Indeed, it could well have been modelled upon the piazza developed by Inigo Jones in the

1630s for the duke of Bedford at Covent Garden. It even had a church placed in relation to the square in the same position as St. Paul's, Covent Garden.[200] Such a scheme, presented as a well-executed drawing, seems to confirm Silvester's metropolitan connexions (Fig. 44). The plan also shows Castle House, larger than it is today, with an impressive flight of steps approaching it from the north; the gatehouse; the 'great mount next to the Wye' in the south-west corner of the Green and 'the mount next to Mrs. Bosworth' – Hogg's Mount. Two un-named passages lead away from the site on the north – the present Quay Street and St. Ethelbert's Lane.

Nothing more is heard of Silvester's plan but in 1696, in a similar spirit of improvement, the city authorities inaugurated a project to construct a waterworks at the Castle Mill so as to bring water into St. Peter's Square. This was a much needed provision as the city was far behind the likes of Worcester and Shrewsbury, which had established 'conduits' much earlier in the 17th century (Fig. 45). Although the common seal of the city was applied to the agreement in May 1696, nothing further was heard of this proposal.[201]

It was the barbican, in the possession of the city, that benefited from the renewed interest in the Wye navigation in the 1690s. Notwithstanding

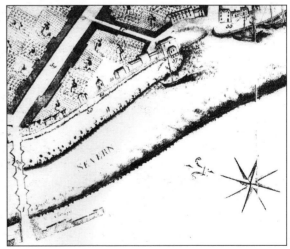

Fig. 45. The waterworks at Worcester (37) from Richard Broad's Plan of the City of Worcester (1768).

their reservations in 1662, the Common Council of the city was amongst the principal backers of the new Navigation Act of 1695. In August 1697 'the waste ground on the east end of the Barmingames … on the backside of the Castle House or Bridewell' was leased to Mr. Church and Mr. Taylor, who had permission to erect buildings. In 1702 they had enclosed it with a wall; in 1725 a wharf was under construction, and when the lease was renewed by Philip Symonds in 1735 the wharf was complete and several buildings had 'lately been erected'.[202] The navigation was immediately beneficial to Hereford and in 1706 the council were seeking the opinion of a solicitor 'respecting the removal of the market' from High Town because the wheat market was much greater than formerly. Apparently the stalls were spreading into the streets around the market house and thus creating a nuisance.[203] The minutes are not very explicit, but surely the council must have once again considered Silvester's proposal for a grain market in the Castle Green.

The city authorities were intent upon removing what remained of the castle mount and a series of grants, beginning in 1724, gave permission to 'all persons to take gravel from the mount there till the same be levelled'. Presumably, the mount was quickly removed, for within a decade the council was reserving the right to dig gravel for its own use. Nevertheless, other grants were periodically made until 1757, when it must be assumed that all traces of the castle hill had been eradicated. The enthusiasm of the city to dispose of the mount encouraged the tenants of Castle Green to do likewise. In 1710, Robert Dobyns is recorded as removing 20 loads of stone 'having wholly pulled down and carried away' the

stone wall on the north end of Castle Green. He also dug up the steps that led to the Green, presumably beside the Bridewell. Dobyns eventually lost his lease, and in July 1712 the magistrates granted it for 42 years to the Hon. James Brydges Esq. for a rent of £8 5s. They were soon to discover that Brydges posed an even greater threat to the public exploitation of the Green than the unfortunate Dobyns.[204]

The Duke of Chandos:
A new 'Box' in Castle Street

James Brydges, later first duke of Chandos, was M.P. for Hereford from 1698 to 1714. His first recorded connection with the castle occurred in a letter he received from Edward Harley in October 1690, which suggests that a 'woollen manufactory' be established on Castle Green, to take advantage of the proposed Act to make the Wye navigable. Brydges was to put the proposal to the county magistrates at the next sessions, but unfortunately ill health prevented Harley from attending.[205] The money for the manufactory was to come from the Scudamore charity, of which Brydges was a trustee. In November 1701 he was accused by James Morgan, the other M.P. for Hereford, of abusing his position as a trustee and

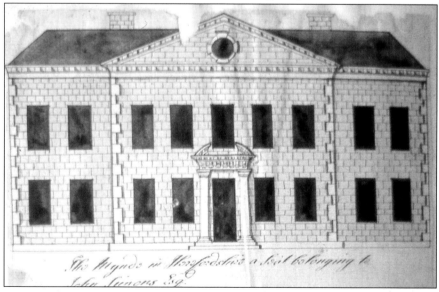

Fig. 46. The Mynde, Much Dewchurch, when James Brydges bought it in c.1720.

56

to clear his name he fought a duel with Morgan on Castle Green. He recorded in his journal:

> After several passes the hilt of my sword struck against the hilt of his & loos'ned it in his hand whereupon I caught hold of it & put it in my sword hand, upon which he clos'd with me & struggled some time; but finding that I must at long run either take away his life, or put him into a condition of taking mine, I chose rather to put both the swords into his hand, & told him that rather than I would take away his life at such an advantage he should have both the swords & my life too. Upon which wee embrac't & both vowed friendship to each other, he din'd with me afterwards as did several other gentlemen, & in the afternoon I went to Mr. Geer's with Mr. Ganderton & Mr. Senhouse.[206]

Brydges had inherited considerable property in south Herefordshire and had assumed the title Viscount Chandos of Wilton. In 1723 he discussed with the architect, Francis Smith of Warwick, a scheme to build a house on the site of Wilton castle, but nothing came of this and subsequently, he bought The Mynde in the parish of Much Dewchurch (Fig. 46).[207] He also had a town house in Hereford, just inside St. Owen Street gate, to which, in 1716, he added additional garden ground at the east end of Castle Street, which was leased from the Vicars' Choral. It was already surrounded on three sides by gardens in Chandos's ownership and appears to have been part of a grand scheme to build a 'box' adjoining the Green, which was revealed in 1726.[208]

In February, Chandos wrote to his cousin, Francis Brydges of Tyberton, describing his intention to build a house of six rooms on each floor in the middle of the present garden. Presumably the 'present garden' was the land that he leased at the east end of Castle Street, bounded on the south by the castle pool and on the east by the city wall (Fig. 47). Taylor's plan of 1757 has this area marked as garden ground, planted sparsely with trees. Later, in April 1726, Chandos wrote again to William Brydges (son of Francis) stating that he had agreed to sell The Mynde and that:

> it will be absolutely necessary for me to have some house in Herefordshire, where Lord Carnarvon or I may have a room to sleep in when we come down to look after our concerns in that county and Radnorshire. I really intend to lay out a sum of five or £6000 in building one, and this will go but a little way towards erecting a seat. I don't know

Fig. 47. A modern aerial view of Castle Green from the north-east. The gardens and ground, now crossed by Cantilupe Street, with the trees of the Green beyond, marks the site of the duke's proposed house and garden.
(Photo: Derek Foxton Collection)

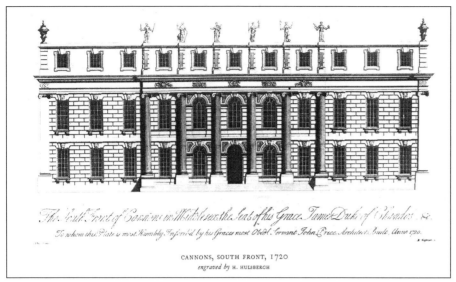

CANNONS, SOUTH FRONT, 1720
engraved by H. HULSBERGH

*Fig. 48. The south front of Cannons in Middlesex c.1720 –
the monumental house of the duke of Chandos.*

another convenient place to build a box upon than that spot of ground, which is at the end of the town, close to the river, and commands a fine prospect all over the country. And as I propose to begin something of this, this summer (if I see a likelihood of having this claim of Harleys cleared up to my satisfaction).[209]

Francis and William Brydges petitioned the magistrates to approach Lord Oxford for a firm conveyance of the Green to the county. This they did, but Lord Oxford was unmoved and clearly reluctant to see a piece of land, bought by his ancestor for the benefit of the county community, pass into private ownership. Moreover, the Harleys had recently run into difficulties with Chandos over the development of their estate in the west end of London.[210] Thus, there was an element of tit-for-tat in their reluctance to clear the legal ground for Chandos to build a new house in Hereford. Edward Harley wrote to his cousin, the earl of Oxford at Wimpole in Cambridgeshire in January 1727: 'I find that Africus [Chandos] stirs in it [that is the attempt to acquire Castle Green], either to get some ground for himself ... or to gain himself a little popularity'. A month later he 'thinks your lordship's

claim should be that it may be a real service to the county and not get into Africus's or other private hands'.[211]

Chandos surrendered his interest in Castle Green in 1735 to Timothy Geers, who appears to have lived at 29 Castle Street. Chandos, instead, built a *pied de terre* at Canon Bridge House, very much the 'box' he envisaged establishing adjoining Castle Green. Today we can only applaud the reluctance of the Harleys to release Castle Green to Chandos. But this is, perhaps, tinged with regret that Hereford lost a house designed by Francis Smith of Warwick or possibly James Gibbs, and terraced gardens, like those at Cannons in Middlesex, so elaborate they stimulated the ire of that arbiter of public taste in early Georgian England, Alexander Pope (Fig. 48).[212]

Towards a public park :
The Society of Tempers

That Chandos should aspire to make Castle Green into private pleasure grounds, suggests that, in the early 18th century, the amenity value of the area was already appreciated by others. Thomas Geers, father of Timothy, who lived in Castle Street, was a sergeant at law and Deputy Steward of the city. In the late 17th century he built two summer houses connected by a raised walk on the boundary of his property overlooking Castle Green (Fig. 49).[213] From there he was able to enjoy a view of the diminishing mount and what was left of the castle. Celia Fiennes, on one of her journeys to Herefordshire in 1696, appears to have climbed the mount, noting that it was 'the only thing of the castle that remains and commands the sight of the river and town'. Moreover, the bishop of Hereford, Lord James

Fig. 49. Two summer houses, built by Thomas Geers, taking advantage of the picturesque prospect of the remains of the fading castle.

Beauclerk (1746-87), the grandson of Nell Gwynne and Charles II, also noticed the green and, according to a mid-18th-century source, provided the patronage for the establishment of the walks. Joseph Jones, writing in 1858, states that Beauclerk laid out the 'admirable and attractive promenade' in 1746 and quotes a poem of 1759, mourning the death of John Philips (1676-1708):

> When Marlborough's triumphs shook the Gallic throne,
> Wye heard a Philips, Thames a Addison:
> Too soon was Philips mourned. O! had he seen
> The present beauties of the Castle Green,
> The Green had flourished in his lasting page,
> And Beauclerk's worth been sung to endless age.[214]

It is possible that in 1748 Beauclerk may have been instrumental in persuading Edward Harley, 4th earl of Oxford, to excuse the Herefordshire magistrates from their £600 debt to his family and 'enfeoff and confirm the property unto his majesties J.P.s' on the understanding that it would remain in public use.

The formal inauguration of the walks is registered in the Quarter Sessions Order Book on October 1752, where it is recorded: 'This court doth as much as it lieth give leave for the making of a commodious walk around the Castle Green',

which also included, according to a later source, permission to take gravel from the castle mount to raise the height of the upper walk. Lord Oxford was present at the meeting and consented to the proposal, which was also welcomed by the 'mayor, corporation and inhabitants of the city of Hereford'.[215] Three years later, the herbage of the Green was granted to Mr. James Terry on condition that he only grazed the area with sheep. Significantly, by 1760, the rights of herbage had passed to Mr. Coldbatch, a founder member of the Society of Tempers – established in 1752 to take over the lease of Castle Green and provide for its management.[216] Originally, the society appears to have had seven members, but by the late 18th century, it was around 40. The *Hereford Guide* (1827) explains that the key objective of the society was for its members 'to enjoy the pleasures of conviviality, and good fellowship'. The *Guide* adds that it had 'considerable standing in the city, and derives its name from the approved tempers of the members, which are tried upon admission; the members are of the first respectability'. Castle Green was taken care of by the Society until its dissolution in 1831.[217]

The poet George Crabbe, in his long poem *The Borough* (1810), celebrates in some detail the various clubs that flourished in the Georgian town. Like the Bucks, the Tempers were:

> ... alert and bold;
> A kind of masons, but without their sign;
> The bonds of union – pleasure, song and wine.
> Man, a gregarious creature, loves to fly
> Where he the trackings of the herd can spy;
> Still to be one with many he desires,
> Although it leads him through thorns and briers.

Crabbe's club, like the Tempers, was a place:

> ... where to their friends in town
> Our country neighbours once a month come down;
> We term it *Free-and-Easy*, and yet we
> Find it no easy matter to be free:
> E'en in our small assembly, friends among,
> Are minds perverse, there's something will be wrong;
> Men are not equal; some will claim a right
> To be the kings and heroes of the night;
> Will their own favourite themes and notions start,
> And you must hear, offend them, or depart.
> Thus it appears these envied Clubs possess
> No certain means of social happiness;
> Yet there's a good that flows from scenes like these –
> Man meets with man at leisure and at ease.

The society was lubricious as well as convivial.[218] It had no meeting house but met regularly at one of the hostelries or coffee houses in the city. An annual venison dinner was held early in November, close to a triad of anniversaries – the Glorious Revolution, Queen Elizabeth's birthday and the Gunpowder conspiracy. Although the society eschewed politics, 'controversy or dispute about party', it was decidedly whig in outlook. The membership was urban and *haute bourgeoise*, drawn from the professional classes of the city including well-to-do tradesmen, doctors and clergymen. There was a small non-resident gentry membership.

On acceptance into the society each member took an oath, whilst consuming a bumper of wine or port, promising to obey the president or vice-president and 'duly regard his verbal orders or censures'. Dr. Francis Campbell, a physician at the infirmary and a founder member, was president for 52 years and, in 1801, to acknowledge his service to the society, the members paid for his portrait to be painted by the fashionable artist, Archer James Oliver (1774-1842).[219] Other officers of the society included the chaplain, bell-ringer, gamekeeper, champion, examiner and interpreter. The champion carried a sword, which he used to measure distances, suggesting that the Tempers played bowls. Significantly, the annual venison dinner was held at the Bowling Green Inn in Bewell Street and on these occasions new members were received.

The examiner and the interpreter played a key role in the initiation ceremonies, which were designed to ascertain if the candidate for membership had a suitable temper. These occasions were meant to be confidential, but a disputed election in 1809, entered in the society's minute book, reveals some of the elaborate role-play that took place at these gatherings. The examiner who, in the early 19th century, was the antiquarian, the Rev. John Duncumb, supervised the proceedings and in particular judged the accuracy of a translation, provided by the candidate, of a sentence in the Welsh language, in which he was aided by the 'interpreter'.[220] A successful candidate was declared by the examiner to be an ancient Briton. The interest in Welsh/Celtic traditions suggests that there may have been some connexion between the Tempers and the Druids, whose Silurian Lodge was founded in 1809. Notwithstanding the attempt by 18th century Welsh writers to claim a monopoly of Celtic virtues and traditions, the gentlemen scholars of Herefordshire saw the Wye valley as an integral part of 'Siluria'. The Tempers, it seems, were tapping into this cultural stream in their initiation ceremonies and when John Duncumb published the first volume of his *History of Herefordshire* in 1804, the title page displayed the 'British' cromlech, Arthur's Stone on Dorstone Hill, as a symbol of the Celtic past in which Herefordshire played a central part.[221] Moreover, Castle Green, with its alternative Celtic names and linked in the *Myvyrian Archaiology* with the Arthurian legends, was a very suitable place for the Tempers to play out their cultural charades.[222] Remarkably, they seemed to know very little about the ancient history of the site they occupied and even the erudite Duncumb knew nothing of the early history of St. Guthlac's minster.

There was no subscription to the society, but members who missed a dinner were 'mulcted' two shillings. In the 1780s an ordinary supper cost each member six pence and a venison dinner two guineas. Absence fines generally provided the society with a small increment, which could be employed to maintain the walks and the green. The county magistrates leased the green to the Tempers for a nominal guinea, but their main source of income for maintenance came from members of the public who paid a subscription to use the walks. The subscription seems to have been variable and in April 1772 Dr. Campbell and his deputy, Mr. Skyrme, appealed for more subscriptions as death had removed many of the original supporters. The accounts were periodically published in the *Hereford Journal* and in 1775 the total subscriptions for the year came to £31 14s. 9d. with £21 of that coming from Sir Richard Symons of The Mynde and three guineas from the bishop, Lord James Beauclerk.[223] The sale of the grass cut from the Green also brought in an addition alsix guineas, and there was thus sufficient funds to repair the 'alcove' attached to the south end of the Bridewell. Much of the work in 1775 was carried out by Mr. Grenour, a plasterer from Presteigne who was also employed by Richard Payne Knight at Downton Castle, where he replaced the stucco and repaired the cornice.[224] The dimensions of the alcove or pavilion were recorded by Edward Knight of Wolverley, Worcestershire on his English tour in 1761 (Fig.

50). It had three arches, separated by two piers, with a pediment above.[225] According to the *Hereford Guide* there was another 'summer house' close to the entrance to the Green from St. Ethebert's Lane. It was said to be 'decayed' and in 1824 was replaced with the Green Keeper's house.[226]

A further set of accounts was published for 1775-9. The alcove, now re-christened the arcade, was again in need of repair, having been 'much injured by the fall of the Bridewell House'. The rails along the terrace – designed in the Chinese-Chippendale style on Powle's prospect of 1778 – were 'nearly decayed' and the wall, perhaps the one that ran from the arcade down to the river, needed repair (Fig. 51). The income for this period was £75 6s. 3d. – nearly all provided by members of the Tempers. Lord James Beauclerk's contribution had been reduced to a guinea and the largest contribution came from the sale of grass to Mr. Abrahall, the innkeeper of the Redstreak in High Town, who paid nine guineas per year. Much painting work, tiling and carpentry had been carried out and the paths re-gravelled. The gardener was William Green, assisted by two weeding women, Mary Prosser and Ann Evans, who received 5s. 6d. for the month of May 1778, to be shared between them. Mr. Green received between £4 and £6 *per annum*.[227] The women kept the paths free of weeds which, according to a lease of 1818, were pitched with gravel, and remained so until the early 20th century – much to the chagrin of women with perambulators.[228]

A final set of accounts was published for the period 1779-82, when the total receipts were £52 12s. 4d. The sale of trees brought in £1 5s. but in 1782 the 'grass

Fig. 50. The pedimented pavilion on the terrace, partly hidden by vegetation, from a painting by F. Jukes (1797).

Fig. 51. George Powle, South-East View of the City of Hereford from Basson (1778).

the Woolhope Club found 21 elms still growing around the Green with an average circumference of 12 feet, which, they suggested, implied a planting date early in the reign of George II (1727-60). They also noted the tradition that the trees had been given to the Tempers by the Rev. Morgan Evans, the vicar of Weobley (1704-39), being transplanted from his garden.

Taylor's plan and a variety of illustrations suggest that they were tiered and stilted, in the fashion prevalent in landscape parks before the picturesque era (Fig. 52). In 1804, the Society was informed that James Russell, the occupier of the Castle Mill, had cut down several trees on the side of the bank adjoining the mill pond and cut the tops off several others. As a result, Russell was brought before the court of King's Bench at the expense of the Society.[230] Occasionally, the magistrates treated the wooded slopes of the

was so much trampled … that the crop was spoiled'. Small sums were spent freshening-up the arcade, weeding, mowing, locking the gate, mending chairs and repairing an iron rake. Mr. Symonds, possibly Thomas Symonds the architect, was given a guinea for taking care of the Green, presumably during the rebuilding of the Bridewell. The author of the accounts states that the lack of income 'plainly evinces the impossibility of keeping the Green in any tolerable condition without further assistance'. The Tempers, he warns, will be raising their subscription for access.[229]

Scenes of Georgian Life on the Green

From a variety of sources it is possible to deduce other aspects of the management of the Green by the Tempers. They were responsible for the tree cover and in 1784 the magistrates agreed that they could take down 'what trees they think proper for ornamenting and improving the Castle Green'. The trees they planted to flank the walks were English elms, much used in contemporary parkland for avenues. Their 'aspiring and tapering growth' – noticed by John Evelyn in *Sylva* (1670) – made them eminently suitable for the confined space on Castle Green. In 1868 the members of

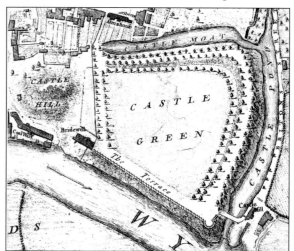

Fig. 52. Taylor's special printing from his Plan of Hereford (1757), showing Castle Green and its environs.

Green, overlooking the Pool, as a separate parcel of land. The value of these inaccessible slopes was presumably the timber/fire wood that grew there. In 1818, for example, they were leased to the Rev. Richard Prosser, archdeacon of Durham, soon to be the owner of Belmont House. The lease, for 31 years at 6d. rent *per annum* stated that 'no soil or filth shall be laid or deposited upon the said piece or parcel of land or any other nuisance committed thereon to the annoyance and inconvenience of persons resorting to the said Castle Green or the public walks'. Significantly, there was no restriction upon the removal or coppicing of the vegetation.[231]

The Green had a beneficial effect upon the neighbourhood, such that a house for sale close to it in 1779 was described as being 'pleasantly situated'. The garden that had been in the possession of the Duke of Chandos was said to extend to the Castle Pool which was 'well stored with fish', and had a dovecote erected on the ruins of the city wall close to where it crossed the Pool.[232] The leaseholders of this desirable piece of water can be traced throughout this period from Timothy Geers in the 1740s, via Francis Woodhouse of Aramston, Chandos's agent and, in 1779, to the surgeon, John Cam, a member of the Tempers, who also seems to have leased an adjoining garden from the Corporation of Hereford for 11s. 6d. *per annum*.[233]

An undated late 18th-century view by James Wathen (Fig. 53) shows many people, mostly couples, walking or seated on the Green, and enjoying the views towards Putson and Dinedor from the 'Terrace' – so named on Taylor's plan of 1757. Half a century later the *Hereford Guide* asserted without qualification that:

> what causes the chief excellence of this walk is the variety of beautiful objects seen from it, which afford delight to every to every spectator, the prospect on every side consisting of the most pleasing and interesting scenery. [The author added that the Wye had recently been] much admired, and particularly described by Gilpin, Ireland and other authors celebrated for their correct taste and enlightened judgement.[234]

The Hon. John Byng, Viscount Torrington, visited Hereford in 1784 and found the 'castle or public walks … well kept'. He returned in 1787 and 'took a turn upon the bridge over the Wye; and then the castle walks, which command a rich prospect, and were more agreeable before the new Infirmary choak'd the view: at one end of the walk are six (not clerical) canons [*sic*]: for the purpose of blowing off arms on rejoicing days'.

The cannons were also noticed by Wathen. As for the Infirmary, for which the first stone was laid on 27 February 1781, the view held locally was that it was an ornament in the landscape. Designed by the city architect/builder, William Parker, its sober Palladian presence was a perfect accompaniment for the classical arcade on the south wall of the Bridewell (Fig. 54).[235]

There are few details of events held on

Fig. 53. James Wathen's view of recreation on Castle Green c.*1800.*

Fig. 54. James Wathen's drawing of the Infirmary and the Bridewell, published by John Price as a frontispiece in his Historical Account of the City of Hereford *(1796).*

the Green during this period. The exception is the announcement on 10 November 1785 that Mr. Dale, a balloonist, would make an ascent from Castle Green. His vehicle was described as 'a great step towards the perfection of Aerostatic Machines'. Tickets were for sale at 5s., 2s. 6d., and 1s. A week later the *Journal* described how Mr. Dale's balloon had exploded because of a 'concussion of internal and external air'. There appear to have been no casualties although there was a large crowd present, many of whom had forced themselves onto the Green without paying.

In warm weather swimming in the river, beneath the cannons placed at the south-east end of the terrace, was a popular recreation for the youth of the city. In August 1802 a youth called Preece was drowned and the report in the *Hereford Journal* mentioned several earlier fatalities.[236]

A less dramatic threat to the harmony of the Green developed in 1787. Access, as now, appears to have been via Quay Street where in 1768 a stile was created 'between the Castle Green and Castle Hill, towards St. Ethelbert's Well'.[237] The narrow passage beside St. Ethelbert's Hospital is mentioned as early as

1589, but it seems to have terminated at the pool where earlier there had been a public washing place.[238] The approach via Quay Street was rendered more salubrious when the city magistrates finally put a stop to the removal of soil and gravel and threatened to fine anyone leaving rubbish there.

Following the collapse of the west tower of the cathedral in 1786, the dean and chapter were looking for a new site for a burial ground for 'the several parishes of the city'. The county justices were sympathetic and a lease was drawn up for the site of the Castle Hill, but a few months later the dean and chapter declined the offer.[239]

Equally detrimental to the ambience of the area were the ambitions of the leaseholder of the Castle Mill. Taylor's plan of 1757 shows a footbridge crossing the mill-stream, giving access to the Bartonsham meadows 'a pleasant walk by the Wye side, which is much frequented in summer', according to the *Hereford Guide*. The bridge is visible on Fisher's view of 1790 (Fig. 55), but in 1797 it was obstructed by rails, posts and a gate.[240] The Common Council ordered the city sergeants and their assistants, the porters, to pull down the barrier. There were further encroachments in 1799. Water-mills were increasingly valued as

Fig. 55. Simon(?) Fisher, View of the Infirmary from Castle Green *(c.1790).*

properties in a picturesque landscape, and several on the Welsh border were painted by the water-colourist, Thomas Hearne, including Hay Mill, sited close to Downton Castle on the Teme. However, millers were engaged in an industrial process and their environmental sensitivity could not always be guaranteed. The cutting down of trees above the mill pool in 1804 was a case in point. Similarly, Mr. Grainger, the tenant at the mill, was prosecuted in 1779 for erecting a pig-cot and creating a nuisance. In dry weather, as in 1775, the mill pool was also likely to dry up causing offensive smells and diminishing its visual contribution to the managed landscape.[241]

Apart from walking in the Bartonsham meadows and pausing to admire the slish-slosh of the mill wheel, it was also possible to hire a plea-sure boat from the Castle Quay for a trip either up or down the Wye. John Easton ran a weekly passenger trow from the Quay to Bristol in the 1820s, and earlier – in May 1793 – Mr. Greenly of the Saracen's Head Inn, was selling a pleasure

boat 'well adapted to rowing or sailing; capable of accommodating twenty persons very comfort-ably, with an awning, neat chequered curtains, full suit of colours … and all her sails and rigging in complete repair'. Such a boat was presumably used in 1798 when a group of gentry, including Uvedale Price and Richard Payne Knight, took a trip down the river during the Three Choirs Festival for a 'music party' at Holme Lacy and, on their way, viewed 'the wild and romantic scenery which adorns the river' (Fig. 56).[242] The Castle Quay, close to the cathedral, would seem to be the most convenient point of departure for this *fête champetre* and the busy commercial activities which took place there were no imped-iment to the enjoyment of the castle walks. Indeed, as contemporary writers on the picturesque frequently pointed out, the daily and routine activities of mankind, when viewed from within a fine landscape, merely served to 'animate the scenery'. J.M.W. Turner's painting of Hereford cathedral (1794) has, as its fore-

Fig. 56. *James Wathen's view of a pleasure boat in the midst of a busy scene on the river at Hereford, c.1790.*

James Biss, who operated the Castle Quay at this time, was prepared to forward 'all sorts of goods … with greatest care and expedition to Chepstow, Bristol and London'. Wine and brandy pipes and puncheons were advertised for sale on the quay in November 1789 and the cathedral surveyor, Thomas Symonds, had his stone yard there.[244] Timber was also very much in evidence and bark for the tanning industry, piled up in stacks, is clearly visible on Wathen's 1793 view of

ground, the Castle Quay, packed with utilitarian structures associated with the river trade and a similar atmosphere is apparent on Edward Dayes' view of 1797 (Fig. 57).[243]

the Bridewell (Fig. 58).[245] Such stacks were much admired by landscape painters in this period and the poet, William Shenstone, whose famous *ferme ornée* The Leasowes near Halesowen was

Fig. 57. *Turner's view of the cathedral and the river Wye*

Fig. 58. James Wathen, North View of the Bridewell and Dinedor Hill *(c.1800),*

all the rage in the late 18th century, thought they were a cheap substitute for temples in an ornamental landscape. The *Hereford Journal*, with a truly sublime eye for pictorial scenes, almost celebrated the fire that broke out among the bark stacks in December 1770: 'the reflection of so large a mass of fire, which was so strong as to communicate light into the rooms of houses very remote from it, all conspired to excite a dread and horror'. Fortunately, 'the wind blew full from the west' and the adjoining buildings were saved.[246]

The Bridewell

The Bridewell or House of Correction, located in the Governor's House (now Castle Cliffe), since the late 17th century, also seems to modern eyes to be an incongruous institution in a picturesque landscape and an unsuitable neighbour for a classical arcade. It was, however, contained within a fragment of the medieval castle, sometimes referred to as the Watergate, with a medieval arch associated (at least from the Georgian era) with Harold Godwinson, the saviour of Hereford in 1055.[247] On Wathen's view of 1793 it looks very much as it does today (Fig. 58). Moreover, polite society in the 18th century was fascinated by felons and paupers – those casualties of early capitalist society – and enterprising gaol keepers could augment their meagre salary by putting the

unfortunates on view. There was something morbidly picturesque about beggars and the like and they often acted as props in contemporary landscape paintings. As Malcolm Andrews has recently pointed out, the picturesque experience in this period was often replete with moral lessons, gained from reflecting upon ancient monuments and the works of nature. It formed an essential part of the pleasures of the imagination, which glutted the mind of the romantically inclined. Notwithstanding these esoteric considerations, the Bridewell was a constant headache for the county magistrates.[248]

A statute of 1607 enacted that houses of correction should be established in every county 'with the necessary implements, to set rogues, vagabonds, sturdy beggars or other idle vagrant and disorderly persons on work'. Several had already been founded in the late 16th century and many more in the early 17th century; thus the Hereford house of correction (or Bridewell, after its precursor in London) was late on the scene.[249] It was built and maintained by the county magistrates, serving the wider community rather than just the city. From the very beginning it was more than a house of correction for the counterfeit poor, for it also provided work and refuge for the deserving poor. The royal surveyor, William Husband, noticed in his extent of 1682 that the

. 59. Criminal activities in the Bridewell at Hereford from The Cry of the Oppressed *(1691)*

sheriff of the county had 'built a work house ... and is about to erect several other houses for the use of the county employing poor people in manufacture there'.[250] Originally, the Bridewell only occupied part of Castle House, but in 1703 the county wished to extend the facilities and two years later the manager of the house of correction, Simon Sheldon, was asked to move 'the prisoners in his custody out of the house in Castle Green' – presumably the south end of the Castle House – where they had been housed temporarily, into the 'new house of correction called old Bridewell now providing and fitting up within the precincts of the common gaol'. From this it is apparent that the Bridewell shared the Castle House with the gaol – a combination condemned by contemporary reformers. Within the building, however, it looks as if the two institutions were kept separate. In 1729 the Bridewell keeper, William Symonds, was sacked for not residing on site and neglecting the poor persons who 'have been like to starve for want of due care'. As a result, the gaol keeper, William Aston, was made responsible for the Bridewell and given the additional title of Master of the House of Correction (Fig. 59).[251]

The building was frequently out of repair during the 18th century, but its role as a penitentiary was diminished with the building of a new county gaol in St. Peter's Square in the early 18th century. This appears to have contained a debtor's prison as well as a house of correction. It occupied the site of the present Shirehall.[252] The old Bridewell continued in use and repairs were carried out in 1735 and 1742, making it 'convenient for the reception of vagrants and other idle and disorderly persons'. In 1747 the ground adjoining the Bridewell, measuring 67 by 38 feet, was leased to Mr. Pyle to erect a warehouse or wharf. Further repairs were carried out in 1754 and the ground to the north-east of the building adjoining the site of the mount, which perhaps had earlier been used as the prison courtyard, was turned into a garden and enclosed. After a dispute over access, it was leased to Thomas Ireland in 1762 and is shown neatly fenced on Wathen's view of 1793 (Fig. 58).[253]

The insecurity of the Bridwell was revealed in 1777 when Edward Rumsey escaped. The magistrates were quick to blame the keeper, Thomas Hill, who was prosecuted and removed from office. He was replaced by William Symonds, a barge owner, who promised not to maintain a public house at the Bridewell. He was granted £10 'to assist him in employing persons committed to the Bridewell', in other words, to purchase materials for the inmates to work upon. In 1779 the Hereford carpenter/builder, Francis Thomas, delivered a plan of repairs for the building, along with an estimate of £120.[254]

At this time the state of the county gaol in St. Peter's Square, established in converted buildings, was also causing concern, and in July 1785 the assize judge, Sir Beaumont Hotham, summoned the grand jury, which condemned the state of the gaol and called a public meeting at the Shirehall to consider repairs and improvements.[255] The result involved considerable expenditure, but it proved inadequate when several felons escaped in 1788. Prompted by this and the criticisms levelled at the gaol by the reformer, John Howard, the magistrates began to consider constructing a purpose-built prison to replace the Bridewell and the miscellaneous buildings in St. Peter's Square.

On Howard's visit to the Bridewell in c.1780 he found half a dozen inmates starving and without water. As for the building this was ruinous, its cross-wall parted from the sidewalls it abutted, with water leaking into the dayroom which had no fireplace and stank of offensive sewers. There was also no yard and the keeper informed Howard that a recent inmate died after only three weeks of confinement.[256]

In 1787/8 plans for a new Bridewell were drawn up by the mason /architect, Thomas Symonds, a monumental sculptor, cathedral artisan and country house builder (Fig. 60). He had previously carried out extensive work on the gaol in St. Peter's Square, as well as the Bridewell, and was probably the most qualified craftsman in Herefordshire at this date. He produced a plan and two watercolour perspectives; one of the existing Bridewell, which shows a good deal more of the medieval surface detail than exists to-day; the other, showing the proposed new building (Fig. 60 & Pls. 5 & 6). Taking his cue from the historic site, this depicts a symmetrical gothic building with a battlemented tower at each end – in all nearly 90 feet in length. The principal windows on the ground and first floors have gothic heads and are linked with flanking square windows in the Venetian style. The towers have a low second storey. The effect is serious and clearly not picturesque, lacking the flair displayed at Downton Castle, where Symonds worked for Richard Payne Knight as his clerk of works.[257]

The plan provided by Symonds shows that little or nothing of the old Bridewell was to survive. The central

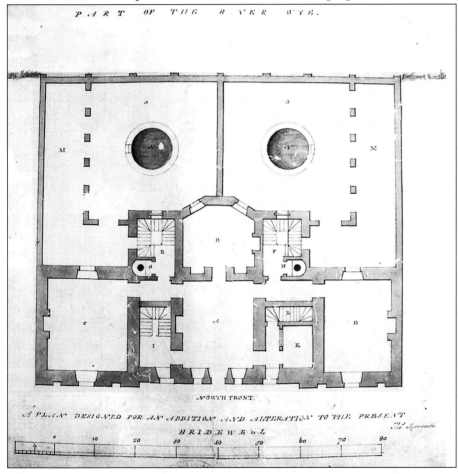

Fig. 60. Thomas Symonds, Plan of the New Bridewell (c.1788).

entrance to the new building gave access to a small hall, beyond which, in the middle of the building, was the keeper's room. This had windows looking out into two courtyards, each provided with 'apartments for labour' along the external walls. On the front of the new building, overlooking Castle Green, were two separate kitchens for male and female prisoners. There were separate 'bogs' and stairs leading down to the chambers in the basement. The first floor provided fairly spacious accommodation for the keeper and his family.

Symonds' scheme was quietly dropped and further extensive repairs were proposed for the principal goal in St. Peter's Square, but in 1790 Howard's protégé, William Blackburn, was commissioned to make plans and estimates for a new purpose-built gaol. Several sites were investigated to ascertain if they satisfied the rigorous criteria laid down by Blackburn and initially he felt that 'the Castle Green has all those requisites, more than any other situation I have seen'. But, he added 'the site of the barbican is deficient … as it is low [and] will be overlooked by the neighbouring houses, the castle walks and high ground, and when encompassed by high walls, will be damp'. Thus, Castle Green narrowly escaped being engulfed by a major county prison and a site at The Priory in Bye Street Without was eventually chosen. Two years later 'Mr. John Nash, architect, in Carmarthen' was called to Hereford to work up the plans and estimates.[258] The prisoners were moved there in July 1796 and in October the old Bridewell, its gardens and appurtenances, were advertised for sale in the *Hereford Journal*.[259]

However, this was easier said than done and once again raised the hoary issue of ownership. Apparently, the documents and papers relating to the castle site, kept in the old gatehouse in a room called The Record, had 'mouldered away' and certain old inhabitants said that 'boys used to break into it and get the parchment to make fireworks'. The county solicitor wrote in 1800 to John Caley of Grays Inn and requested that he carried out a search for the original grant by the crown for Castle Green. Caley responded saying that he had found nothing in the Augmentation Office or among the 'rolls' but provided a copy of the Parliamentary Survey of 1652. He charged a search fee of £2 5s. 4d. and promised to make a further search. This correspondence also indicates that the magistrates still sent £20 annually to Lord Somers, presumably as some sort of ground rent for the castle that was still owed to the crown. But, satisfied with their tenure, the Bridewell was once again put up for auction in September 1800 at the New Inn, Widemarsh Street. It was sold to Mr. Hawker on condition that the access into the Green, running beside the building, should be 'carried under the garden walls' – under arches?

The magistrates, it seems, were at this date considering the outright sale of the Green, but were in dispute with the city council over Castle Hill. They sought a higher opinion from H. Leyster, a barrister, who concluded that the county had a better title to Castle Hill than the city, but both had established rights of access over a long period. The matter was left unresolved for the time being and the magistrates appear to have given up the idea of selling the Green.[260]

St. Ethelbert's Well

Perhaps the most ancient site within the castle precincts was the well or fountain of St. Ethelbert. The earliest reference to this holy site occurs in the boundary clauses of a grant of land on the east side of the close, made by a benefactor to the Dean and Chapter in 1250. The parcel of ground is said to lie towards the '*fontem beati Ethelberti*', which was situated immediately to the north of the castle mount.[261] With the decline of the castle in the early 14th century, Bishop Swinfield appears to have constructed a stone canopy over the well for the convenience of pilgrims who were coming to Hereford in increasing numbers to visit the shrine of St. Thomas Cantilupe. The structure is depicted on Speede's plan of 1610, sketched by Dineley

(1684) and subsequently by Stukeley in 1721 (Figs. 61 & 62). Dineley shows the superstructure in good condition with water flowing towards the river, whilst Stukeley found it ruinous but still protected by a 'handsome stone arch'.[262] Further antiquarian interest before the early 19th century is rare and references to it in the 18th century – the age of reason – are generally in passing. Taylor fails to even record it on his town plan of 1757. Nevertheless, in 1763 the City Council gave permission to a Mr. Maddox to wall in part of the waste ground at the barbican, but insisted that he leave the way to St. Ethelbert's well open 'for public resort as usual'. Later, in 1780, the Improvement Commissioners connected the culverts from Castle Street into 'the drain leading from St. Ethelbert's Well to the river'. Consequently, they seem to have assumed responsibility for its upkeep and gave instructions to cleanse it in 1782.[263]

In 1801 a plan drawn up prior to the building of St. Ethelbert House, (Fig. 63) shows the well as a circular feature surrounded by walls and approached by steps from Castle Hill.[264] The stonework about the well had 'recently [1806] been repaired at the expense of Mrs. Joanna Whitworth', at which date, it was still visited by 'persons afflicted by ulcers and sores of various kinds'.[265] John Pyndar Wright (1819) noticed that 'the limped stream' still flowed and 'was much esteemed for its medicinal properties'. Some disjointed remains of the arch described by Stukeley still remained on either side of a door in the wall. Above this was a keystone ornamented with foliage. In a niche above the well was a crowned head of St. Ethelbert, removed from the west front of the cathedral and protected by an iron grille – all part of Mrs. Whitworth's restoration. The water had probably been contaminated by the drainage of Castle Street and careless people threw rubbish into it. Nevertheless, it was still frequented by people from the city and perhaps beyond, for when it was cleaned out, capped and provided with a pump at this time, a great number of votive pins were found.[266] It seems likely, from the above description and the 1801 plan, that the well being referred to is now in the garden of Well Cottage, Quay Street, where a stone inscribed 'Well' in fine letters with serifs, has been let into an adjoining wall (Fig. 64).[267] In 1822 the water was analysed by Mr. J. Murray who found that it had a stable temperature of 52° and contained some 'super carbonate of lime, muriate of magnesia and alum'. He concluded that it was not especially medicinal.[268]

However, the water from the spring continued to flow in its culvert, entering the river close to the Bridewell where there was a spout and beneath it a stone basin or cistern which was reached by a flight of steps. In 1827 it had

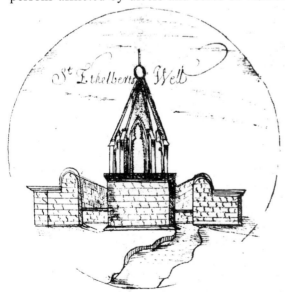

Fig. 61. St. Ethelbert's Well drawn by Thomas Dineley in c.1684.

Fig. 62. The Well as seen by Stukeley in c.1720.

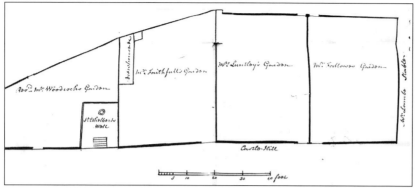

Fig. 63. The site of St. Ethelbert's Well, 1801.

recently 'been put in order' and was said to be useful for 'gravelly complaints'. 'Elderly parties will walk long distances to make use of it', reported the author of *Hereford, Cathedral and City* (1858), and a decade or so later a correspondent in the *Hereford Times* also recorded that a 'number of old inhabitants of the city still go down at early morn to quaff a draught of the water to obtain some of it to cure weak eyes'.[269] From 1830 the more genteel residents of the city could enjoy the water by bathing in the facilities provided beneath the Castle Green Reading Room and in the 1860s the proprietor of the Hereford Brewery, Charles Watkins, considered

Fig. 64. In the garden of Well Cottage, Quay Street. On the wall, a stone with the word 'Well' is carved with some finesse.

bottling the water. However, following further analysis, he abandoned the idea as it was found to be badly polluted by seepage from the city sewers. The cistern beneath the Bridewell was presumably destroyed soon after this and in 1904 the present cast iron drinking fountain was erected by Mr. A. Steel, who also marked the original well with a 'circular stone'.[270] In 1978 the fountain was connected to the mains water supply by the Hereford Civic Trust, who had the stonework restored by Mr. Bigglestone, a stonemason employed by Messrs. Beavan and Hodges. The fountain was rededicated by the Right Rev. J.R.G. Eastaugh, the bishop of Hereford, on St. Ethelbert's day, 20 May 1978 (Fig. 65).[271]

Nelson's Column

Lord Nelson's heroic progress through south Wales and the borderlands in the summer of 1802, accompanied by Sir William and Lady Hamilton, the Rev. William Nelson (the admiral's brother) and his wife, was noticed by the readers of the *Hereford Journal* long before the party entered Herefordshire. The civic leaders of Hereford, conscious of the wonderful reception Nelson had received at Ross and Monmouth and not wanting to be upstaged, hastened to Rudhall Court on Sunday 22 August to invite the admiral to Hereford.[272] The owners of Rudhall, Mr. & Mrs. Thomas Westphaling, were repaying the Hamiltons for the hospitality they had received at Naples during

Fig. 65. The Well in c.*1980 seen in the distance below St. Etherbert House from the Redcliffe Gardens, which were developed in the 1960s on the site of the castle mount.*

their tour of Italy. The party was *en route* for Downton Castle in north Herefordshire to visit another old friend of Hamilton, Richard Payne Knight.[273] A lunch stop at Hereford on their way made good sense and so, on Monday 23 August the party arrived in the city, where the hero of the Nile and Copenhagen was 'met with demonstrations of joy to which his transcendent merit duly entitled him'. The young men of the city unhitched the horses of his carriage and delivered him to the City Arms, from whence, accompanied by the Chief Steward of the City, Charles Howard, 11th duke of Norfolk, the owner of Holme Lacy, he walked to the Town Hall in High Town (Figs. 66 & 67).

Mr. Lambe, the Town Clerk, had the irksome task of making the address and, rather bravely, congratulated Nelson for his victories that had raised the country to 'a pitch of glory' which he had himself selflessly ascribed to the work of God. The corporation's prize for Nelson was the freedom of the city, inscribed upon a box made

'of that tree which is the pride of the county' – apple-wood. As usual Nelson responded by generously praising his officers and men, who demonstrated the 'inbred spirit of the Britons' in repelling enemy attacks. The Rev. Mr. Morgan proffered an apology for the absence of Bishop John Butler at the reception on the grounds of his ill health, but Nelson, perhaps suspecting that the bishop was using this as an excuse not to be in the presence of Lady Hamilton, jokingly offered to call at the palace. The formalities over, the party returned to the City Arms where, as far as is known, Lady Hamilton did not give one of her impromptu concerts of patriotic songs, such as had overwhelmed the townsmen of Monmouth a few days earlier. At 2.00 p.m., after being viewed by many of the population of Hereford as they had their lunch, the party set out for Downton Castle.[274]

Nelson's visit and his acceptance of the freedom of the city ensured that he had a special place in the hearts of the Herefordians. Perhaps

Fig. 66. Lord Nelson by Samuel Lane c.1804.

Fig. 67 Emma Hamilton as Miranda by George Romney, 1786.

some of them also knew of his flattering reference to the men of the county, made as an aside at Monmouth, where he speculated that if the French landed 'they might burn Monmouth – but I will engage for it they would never advance as far as Hereford, for they would always find Britons ready to receive them'. Thus, when it was learnt on 7 November 1805 that Nelson had fallen at Trafalgar, the editor of the *Hereford Journal*, amidst his effusions of patriotic regret, could not resist referring to Nelson's earlier visit to the city and the freedom he had received. Somehow it made the sadness felt for his heroic death more poignant, and out of this sense of personal loss came the proposal to erect an 'obelisk' (Fig. 68).[275]

On Saturday 9 November the city was illuminated by bonfires and volleys were fired by the Herefordshire Volunteers, but the bells were muffled at the loss of one of England's 'brightest ornaments'. The *Journal* announced that a subscription was being raised in the city and its neighbourhood for 'the purpose of evincing our respect towards the memory of the gallant Nelson'. An 'obelisk of Bath stone, surmounted by an urn, defended by iron railings might be erected' at the centre of Castle Green. Remarkably, the full inscription had already been composed and was printed in the paper. Within a week the subscription had reached £100 and a committee of gentlemen had been established to further the project. However, Herefordshire's enthusiasm for its own 'obelisk' was slightly diminished by the knowledge that a subscription had been opened for a national monument and, moreover, a patriotic fund had been established for 'the heroes who suffered in the late glorious action'. The editor of the *Journal* agreed the latter was a good cause and suggested that part of the Herefordshire subscription could be diverted to support it. More disturbing was a letter from a 'Volunteer', who dismissed the Castle Green obelisk on the grounds that it had been 'conceived in haste' and would not do justice to Nelson's achievement.

Friday's Post.

London Gazette Extraordinary.

DESTRUCTION

OF THE

Combined Fleets of France and Spain,

AND

The Death

OF

LORD NELSON !!!

ADMIRALTY-OFFICE, NOV. 6.

DISPATCHES, of which the following are copies, were received at the Admiralty-Office this day, at one o'clock, A. M. from Vice-Admiral Collingwood, Commander in Chief his Majesty's ships and vessels off Cadiz.

Sir,   *Euryalus, off Cape Trafalgar, Oct.* 22.
The ever to be lamented death of Vice Admiral Lord Viscount Nelson, who, in the late conflict with the enemy, fell in the hour of victory, leaves me the duty of informing my Lords Commissioners of the Admiralty, that on the instant, it was communicated to the Commander in Chief from the ships watching the motions of the enemy in Cadiz, that the combined fleet had put to sea; as they sailed with light winds westerly, his Lordship concluded their destination was the Mediterranean, and immediately made all sail for the entrance of the Streights, with the British squadron, consisting of twenty-seven ships, three of them sixty-fours, where his Lordship was informed by Captain Blackwood (whose vigilance in watching, and giving notice of the enemy's movements, has been highly meritorious) that they had not yet quitted the Streights.
On M—

Fig. 68. Headlines in the Hereford Journal *for 7 November 1805.*

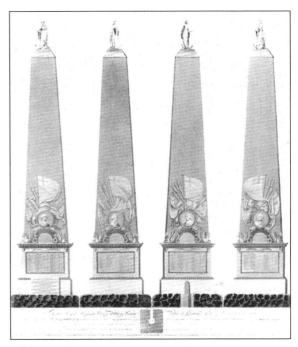

Fig. 69. Obelisk proposed for Pottsdown Hill, Portsmouth following the battle of the Nile, 1799.

He suggested that the enthusiasm of the nation should not be dissipated and scattered in providing for 'a bauble fit to ornament the narrow grass plot of a suburban villa', rather that the Herefordshire subscription should be used to support the national monument. The editor dismissed this idea on the grounds that the designs of the Hereford monument had yet to be settled and that local subscribers were unlikely to visit London (Fig. 69).[276]

By 11 December the Hereford subscription had reached £350, but the patriotic fund was also well supported as it was collected on a parish-by-parish basis. The corporation of Hereford gave the latter £50, the former £21; clearly there was a moral imperative to support those 'maimed in the service of the country'. Nevertheless, the *Journal* stated that 'work will immediately be put into a state of forwardness' for the obelisk. The 'Volunteer', however, was far from satisfied and threw further scorn upon the 'multiplication of obelisks from Caithness to Cornwall … [these] scattered effusions of patriotism'. He was personally prepared to contribute to a votive tablet erected locally but not a 'folly'. Some readers of the *Journal* would perhaps, have seen his point on learning that £2000 had been raised for the Birmingham obelisk. But the Hereford project survived and on 18 December it was announced that the local subscription had reached £400 and the committee of gentlemen had received 'two excellent designs furnished by Mr. Hardwick, archt. of London'. One of these had been selected.[277]

Thomas Hardwick (1752-1829) had travelled extensively in Italy with the Welsh artist, Thomas Jones, between 1776 and 1779. He was also an early partner of one of the most talented and original architects of the period, John Soane, and employed J.M.W. Turner in his office before he took up painting. He was 'an accomplished draughtsman and competent designer' – evidenced by several surviving handsome churches.[278] He was also well known in Hereford, having provided a structural survey of the surviving portion of the cathedral after the collapse of the west end in 1786, whilst at the same time advising upon the state of All Saints' spire, where he proposed a new tower.[279] Later, in 1812, he was to submit designs for the new Shirehall, but they were rejected in favour of those by Sir Robert Smirke. A rough sketch of the obelisk, presumably prepared for a print, exists in the Pilley Collection in the City Library. It shows a crudely drawn classical figure on the top (Fig. 70).[280]

On 1 January 1806, the committee published a notice in the *Journal* providing details of the obelisk. It was to have a circular column of either Bath or Portland stone; to be 4 feet in diameter and 52 feet high; and the base or 'altar' was to be 12 feet square. The fund was said to be equal to the task, but the public were to decide 'by their generosity' upon a statue or an urn. The former would cost 100 guineas, the latter only 30. The Hereford banks were ready to receive further subscriptions. In some quarters, there were still signs of discontent with the proposal and one correspondent suggested that

a temple and a statue would be better than a column.[281]

Thomas Wood, a prolific monumental mason who had taken over the business of Thomas Symonds in Church Street next to the cathedral

Fig. 70. 'A private etching of the intended column in Castle Green' with an indistinct signature – possibly 'T. Wood 1805'.

Fig. 71. Winkles, Hereford Cathedral from Castle Green *(1842).*

close, was chosen to execute the design and on 29 January 1806 it was announced that work on the obelisk had commenced; the first stone being laid on Wednesday 2 April. The ceremony was attended by the three local lodges of the Masons, the first regiment of the Herefordshire Volunteers and a 'large concourse of freemen'. Speeches were made, volleys fired and 150 people attended a celebratory dinner at the City Arms. The editor of the *Journal* concluded that the 'monument will perpetuate his patriotism and noble deeds, to admiring posterity'.[282]

The financial accounts for the obelisk or 'columnal monument', as the *Hereford Guide* called it, were published in August 1809 and March 1812. Hardwick's design was apparently altered by Thomas Wood and this required more

carving and mason's work leaving a deficit of £38 in 1809. This had risen to £190 16s. 9d. in 1812 when the expensive carvings, including five dolphins, a bust, cables, torches, cornice and other mouldings, were itemised. The principal inscription was carved on a tablet by Thomas Late, one time assistant to William Parker, the architect of the General Hospital and chief mason at John Nash's new County Gaol. The final touch was to be provided by iron railings, purchased from Mr. J. Parker of Stourport for £56.[283] However, these are lacking on the lyrical engraving by Winkles, dated 1842, where the column rises from a flowery knoll, accompanied on one side with vigorous shrubs (Fig. 71). Along with the new temple on the south-east façade of the Bridewell, it contributed a further picturesque ingredient to Castle Green, adding a touch of solemnity to the Georgian pleasure grounds.[284]

Residents and visitors alike took pride in this 'patriotic memorial' and guidebooks and directories were keen to point out that it was paid for entirely from voluntary subscriptions from the city and neighbourhood. It was eventually enclosed with iron railings in 1857 when the cannons, including Roaring Meg, which had been placed on the bastion at the south end of the terrace by Bishop Beauclerk, were clustered here

Fig. 72. Rook & Co., London, Nelson Monument on Castle Green *(c.1855).*

for fear that their weight would endanger the river bank. The M.P. for Herefordshire, Sir Joseph Bailey, paid for the work and the results were illustrated in 1855 (Fig. 72).[285] There were still some dissenting voices complaining about the design, as in 1875 when an anonymous correspondent of the *Hereford Times* referred to it as a 'huge inverted fungus' and a blot upon the 'natural and artificial beauty of its surroundings'. The same writer applauded the demolition of the 'dilapidated, rickety and patched up old building used as a Town Hall, which disgraced the middle of High Town'. 'A Native Citizen' responded with a spirited defence of the column, which

'although not a high work of art, is by no means a monstrosity, or an uninteresting or inelegant feature in this grand and beautiful public ground'. This was very much the majority view.[286]

The Demise of the Tempers

During the Regency period the beauties and amenities of Castle Green were much celebrated in a spate of guidebooks and visitors' journals. With the middle classes fully engaged in the pursuit of the picturesque; living in a society where painting and writing poetry were regarded as normal accomplishments for members of the polite classes, it was inevitable that walking, strolling and tourism became an essential ingredient of the well-tempered life.[287] This trend was to be accentuated as the 19th century progressed with the universal acceptance of evangelical piety, which took the edge off the Georgian *joie de vie* but made walking and visiting the park a godly, or at least, a morally neutral activity. The 1830s saw a number of new urban parks created, promoted by men with a deep religious conviction who, with benevolent intentions, wished to tame the anarchic inclinations of the burgeoning working classes.[288]

John Price (1772-1801), a young peripatetic language teacher from Leominster who understood the landscape better than many of his contemporaries, wrote the best appreciation of Castle Green in the *Historical Account of the City of Hereford* (1796), which was copied and slightly amended in subsequent editions of the *Hereford Guide*. Price wrote:

> It would be unpardonable here, not to mention a very elegant public walk south-east of the city, called Castle Green, being the

Fig. 73. Part of a view from Putson, published by W.H. Vale in December 1825. The Georgian pavilion is fading and the walks are in an 'objectionable state'.

site of an ancient castle; at first formed, and kept in neat order by the corporation. It has been esteemed superior to any other walk of the kind in the kingdom: but taste, unimproved by attention and study, varies more perhaps in scenery and landscape, than it does upon any other subject. The walk is nearly quadrangular, having the Wye, a large and beautiful river, gliding by it on the south. Towards the north and east, this walk is formed into an outer and inner one. The inner one is shaded with a row of elms, which are literally, according to the poet, 'From storms a shelter, and from heat a shade' The outer walk rises by an ascent of twelve or fifteen feet above the other, and appears to have been the keep and part of the wall of the castle, not quite levelled. From this outer walk you see a moat below, partly encompassing the site of the castle, which is always full of fresh water, and abounds in carp and other kinds of fish. But what constitutes the chief excellency of this walk, is the variety of beautiful objects seen from it, which must strike the admiration of every curious traveller, who chooses to visit it.[289]

Notwithstanding this warm encomium, the Society of Tempers was finding difficulty in maintaining the Green. In 1807 they established a committee 'to examine the present state of the Castle Green and make a report thereon'. Estimates to 'put the walks in proper order' were prepared for March 1808, but very little seems to have been done. The Society itself was languishing, its meetings became less frequent and in 1817 the annual dinner – for so long the climax of the Temper's social calendar – was cancelled.[290] The clubbable and bibulous Georgian world was being undermined by a new sense of seriousness, which began to pervade society. James Wathen, the gregarious local artist, also found the atmosphere in Hereford changing in the first decades of the 19th century, blaming evangelicalism, which sowed discord among his friends, 'severing the firmest intimacies'.[291] The demise of the Tempers perhaps reflects this process. With declining membership and little income the Society was incapable of maintaining the walks. The problem was expressed succinctly in their minute book on the great Whig festival of 5 November 1818:

> It having been a subject of much regret among the inhabitants of this city and its neighbourhood, that the Castle Green walks and premises should remain in so objectionable a state, arising chiefly from the wilful destruction which every improvement hitherto attempted has met with, and partly from a want of a regular method to preserve the same; it was suggested this day by the Society of Tempers that some effectual means should be adopted, as well to preserve the property under lease to themselves, as to afford the public the advantage of enjoying the promenade.[292]

It was proposed that a public subscription be raised from the inhabitants of the city for the purpose of paying the wage of a 'green-keeper' and that the alcove be 'converted into a neat cottage to be tenanted by a neat respectable man' (Fig. 73). The following March plans and estimates were being sought for a cottage of four rooms 'with a veranda sufficiently capable to furnish shelter from the rain and heat'. Mr. Cooke was to undertake this business and obtain the assistance of 'Mr. Heather or any other competent architect'. This was Charles Heather, an assistant of John Nash, who arrived in Hereford in 1812 as the clerk of works to Sir Robert Smirke, the architect chosen to design and build the new Shire Hall (1815-17).[293]

The Society struggled on for another three years, but in 1822 the lease for the Green was due for renewal and it was decided that 'the endeavours made by this Society towards the improvements of the Green having proved abortive, it was unanimously resolved that no renewal of the lease be sought'. On 4 November 1831 the five surviving officers of the society recorded in the minute book that as the lease for Castle Green was not renewed there 'does not now exist an ostensible cause for continuing these meetings; the members present unanimously resolved that the Society be discontinued'. A brief postscript was added, probably in the hand of John Duncumb, present at the meeting, to the effect that, those present:

> cannot however record their resolution without adverting to certain facts and recalling to their recollection the many agreeable days that they have uniformly experienced in carrying into effect the customs and rules of the Society which has existed in the city of Hereford during a period of four score years and which has had the honour and satisfaction of enrolling amongst its members – the names of the most remarkable and respectable inhabitants of the city and its neighbourhood.

Already in 1824 the county magistrates had resolved to grant a new lease for Castle Green 'to the gentlemen of the committee for soliciting subscriptions for the improvement thereof'.[294]

CHAPTER VI

Recreation : The 19th century

The Castle Green Reading Room and Baths Committees

'The gentlemen of the committee' appear to have succeeded in fulfilling the final aspiration of the Tempers, namely to raise a public subscription to demolish the Georgian alcove and build a green keeper's cottage with a veranda looking south-eastwards, down the terrace. In addition, the water from St. Ethelbert's well was piped into a bath suite, above which was a reading room with a bay window overlooking the river. All this was completed by 1830 when the 'gentlemen' split into the committee for Castle Green, and the Reading Room and Baths committee. The transactions of the Green committee have disappeared, but some accounts and minutes for the latter survive from 1830 to 1859.[295]

The new veranda, much like its predecessor the alcove, is revealed on prints and postcards of the 19th century (Fig. 74). Seen from the south-east across the Green it virtually obscured the old Bridewell, being a substantial temple-like structure with four square-sectioned columns under a pediment. Adjoining it, but closer to the river, were the baths and reading room, which were contained within a two-storey building with sash windows on both floors under a moulded pediment. The ground floor was decorated with pilasters and thus echoed the adjoining temple. The complete ensemble was treated with white stucco. Today, the reading room and baths survive (with the addition of a 1960s extension), but the temple has lost its pediment and its colonnade has been under-built. Presumably, as there was insuf-

Fig. 74. The Reading Room and the refurbished 'verandah' in the late 19th century.

Fig. 75. Pool Cottage, now The Fosse.

ficient room in the pavilion, the committee also built a 'convenient residence … for the occupation of a constable, who should take care of the Green'. This was constructed, close to the entrance from St. Ethelbert's Lane, in the north-west corner of the Green, where a 'decayed summer house' stood. The new house, a modest brick affair, had its back to Castle Hill – there was a boundary here in the 18th century – and overlooked the gate which gave access from Castle Street. The new committee, remembering the difficulties faced by the Tempers, decided to lock the gate to the Green at night, but the constable/watchman was to let people through who had business at the Infirmary.

The architect of the new buildings was presumably Charles Heather, who had been chosen by the Tempers before their dissolution. As the local assistant of Sir Robert Smoke he was no doubt also involved in the building of Pool Cottage (now The Fosse), at the north-west end of the Castle Pool between 1824-5 (Fig. 75). This piece of Jacobean revivalism was designed for Captain Pendegrass, a friend of the local artist, James Wathen.[296] The Fosse, St. Ethelbert's

Hospital (also rebuilt in 1805), the Green Keeper's house and the new Reading Room completed the Regency make-over of Castle Green and added to its luminosity as one of the most polished public spaces in the kingdom.

The Reading Room joined two other 'subscription newsrooms' in the city. It was provided with a number of London and provincial papers such as *The Times, The Bath and Cheltenham Gazette* and *The Naval and Military Gazette.* In 1848 the annual bill for these papers came to £33 8s. 3d. Readers included the 'shareholders' who were approved by the committee and paid an unspecified one-off fee for their share. There was 33 in 1830. Of inferior status were the subscribers who paid £1 *per annum* for men and 5s. for women. Strangers not resident in the city could have admission to the Reading Room for a short period if recommended by a shareholder. Papers were stamped 'Castle Green Reading Room' and were strictly prohibited from being carried beyond the room and out onto the Green. When out-of-date, old papers were recycled, which in 1849 raised £2 19s. In 1853 the room was open from 8 a.m. to 9 p.m. except on Sundays when it closed at dusk. Lamps, candles and coals for heating were regular items of expenditure, especially in winter. The room was comfortably furnished with cocoanut matting, painted chairs and sofas, which were occasionally reupholstered. In 1848 the room was completely redecorated at a cost of £26. An attendant looked after the readers, making them sign in to prevent strangers using the facility. There was a 15 minute limit on the possession of a paper and members who acted 'ungentlemanly' were asked to withdraw by the attendant.

The warm baths beneath the Reading Room appear to have been an afterthought and were promoted by the *Hereford Journal* in August 1824. The editor claimed that they could be created at small expense and would be valuable for both invalids and the general public. Apparently all the neighbouring towns had them and were found to be of 'great utility'. Within two weeks of this notice, shares of £5 were available and the warm baths were soon under construction.[297] In 1829 the *Hereford Times* announced that the baths were open and 'the rules for the regulation of the baths and reading room may be seen at the keeper's house'. The room was finished with Spode and Copeland tiles with separate areas for ladies and gentlemen. Far fewer women seemed to use the facility and in 1830 'objectionable persons' were found using the ladies' bath and were ordered by the attendant back to the gentlemen's area. Subscribers to the Reading Room automatically had access to the baths, which could be booked in advance. Nevertheless, they paid one shilling for a bath and six pence for a shower. In 1845 a 'vapour bath' was added. Sunday was clearly a less popular day and any person producing a medical certificate, countersigned by a committee member, was allowed to have a free bath. Presumably these were citizens drawn from the lower classes. To attract more bathers, special discounts were offered in 1846 for booking six baths at once. Candles would be provided free. The idea of a late evening vapour bath in the vaults under the old castle, illuminated only by candles, sounds particularly gothic; no wonder few women took up the offer! William Collins indicates that it was 'quite common for the judges on circuit' to use the baths, presumably after a heavy day sentencing poor people to death or transportation.[298] Perhaps as a result of declining numbers, the committee decided to advertise the baths in the local inns. Nevertheless, in 1849 the income from the baths was only £14 1s. for the year.

In 1853 the subscription for the baths and reading room rose by 50% from 10s. *per annum* to 15s. and the following year it was noted in the minutes that subscribers were withdrawing in protest at the management of the Reading Room. New rules were issued, but this did not stop the decline and in February 1856 a special meeting of the shareholders was called to defray the treasurer's deficit of £24 7s. Later in the year another meeting was called and further measures were taken to reduce expenditure. Fewer papers were taken and the Reading Room was to close at dusk. A 10s. subsidy was requested from subscribers for necessary repairs, but several gentlemen refused to contribute and in January 1857 the treasurer resigned.[299]

The Hereford Literary and Philosophical Institute

A new source of support for the Reading Room and Baths Committee was soon found. In April 1858, after a brief courtship, the committee was subsumed by the Hereford Literary and Philosophical Institute, which in turn was an amalgamation in 1836 of the Herefordshire Natural History, Philosophical, Antiquarian and Literary Societies. The Institute had hitherto occupied rooms above the Gloucester Bank in Broad Street, where it had a library and museum. Acquiring the Reading Room and Baths at a nominal rent of 1s. per year, with a 69 year lease from the county magistrates still to run, appeared to be a God-sent opportunity for the Institute to acquire a new base in surroundings that were more in keeping with its various interests. As the surviving shareholders of the Reading Room were to enjoy all the privileges of the Institute on the payment of 5s. per annum, the proposal was formally accepted at their final meeting on 17 June 1858.[300]

The new society – now generally known as the Literary and Philosophical Society – printed a pamphlet describing their objectives. These were to promote the arts and sciences by means of lectures; to establish a museum of specimens of nature, antiquity, science and art; and to collect a library of general literature. Members became 'shareholders' by paying an annual fee of 15s. Thus, the society embarked upon its activities with great enthusiasm, raising £250 as a mortgage on the building to finance the establishment of its museum and library. It began publishing transactions, which enshrined the lectures given by eminent specialists in the old reading room. The museum, according to one critic, contained 'sundry stuffed animals, one pair, at least, of boots supposed once to have graced the feet of Cromwell, a stuffed creature imagined to be a monkey and similar valuable relics of the past ages'. The library also contained rarities, including an early copy of one of Shakespeare's plays, which was soon to be sold to defray the debt that was about to engulf the society and stifle its activities.

As time passed, the baths fell into disrepair; the museum attracted few visitors and the library 'scantily provided with papers', proved unattractive. Unlike its predecessors, the Tempers and the Reading Room Committee, the Literary Society seemed incapable of making arrangements to wind-up its activities tidily. In 1869 the building was closed, subscriptions went uncollected and the interest on the mortgage increased, with the result, that the mortgagee threatened to destrain upon the contents of the museum to settle his debt. Fortunately, in 1875, the City Council came to the rescue. The building and its contents were transferred to the Council who, in turn, settled the debts of the society.[301] The contents were subsequently given to the new Museum and Free Library in Broad Street, which had been opened in October 1874. This building also contained the meeting room and library of the Woolhope Naturalists' Field Club, many of whose members had originally supported the Literary and Philosophical Society. Along with Dr. Bull and the Rev. W.S. Symonds they found that the latter was uninterested in natural history and thus, the Woolhope Naturalists' Field Club was founded in April 1852, contributing considerably to the slow demise of the older Society.[302]

The Management of the Green 1824-73
Although, the minutes of the Castle Green Committee seem to have disappeared, much can be gleaned from other sources and, indeed, the

Reading Room Committee, who contributed to the wages of the green keeper, were clearly interested in the wider setting of their activities. One such issue was the state of the Castle Pool. As the latter declined into a putrid lagoon, made up almost entirely from the city's waste-water, there was a growing demand for action, not least from the subscribers to the Castle Green amenities. Dredging and removing centuries of accumulated silt, which gave off 'pestiferous odours' in the summer, and increasing the natural flow, were hoped to provide a solution. It became the first objective of the newly formed Green Committee in 1824. The tenants and landowners surrounding the pool, including Captain Pendegrass of The Fosse, were persuaded to contribute and the committee assured its own subscribers that the project would not be a drain on their resources and would even make a profit. There were high hopes that selling the 'manure' would raise at least £100, but in the event only £46 0s. 3d was recovered, and much of this had to be used to compensate the owner of the Castle Mills for the stopping of the water.[303]

Dredging was only a temporary solution to the problem and in 1844 the operation was repeated. Less than ten years later the Public Health Report of 1853 again highlighted the problem of the 'offensive open ditches' around the city and the 'stench of the Castle Mill Pond [which] is abominable in the summer'. The solution was provided by the City Engineer, Thomas Curley, who wrote:

> Now if the abominations above referred to were caused to pass into the sewers instead of the brook, the Castle Pond might be made into an ornamental piece of water; a 'fountain' supplied from the water works, might be erected in its centre at very little expense; and a walk constructed along its edge, a few feet above its water level. This would add another attraction to Castle Green and render it one of the most beautiful public walks in Europe.[304]

Sadly, Curley's aspirations for Castle Green were not immediately fulfilled. Swans were introduced onto the pool for ornamental effect in

1832, but the birds began to multiply and cause a nuisance so steps were taken to remove them.[305] Eventually, main sewers were introduced in 1854 and the Eign Brook was diverted away from the city ditch. The leaseholder of the Castle Mills was compensated and the ditch filled in, including the stretch of the Castle Pool on the eastern side of the Green.[306] Little seems to have been done to the Green itself, which was still grazed by sheep to keep the grass down and generally had the appearance of a rough meadow. However, in 1855, when it became apparent that the Reading Room Committee was about to collapse and their contribution to the wages of the green keeper would cease, a special public meeting was called to discuss the future of the Green and it was resolved that:

> It is most desirable that the Castle Green, one of the chief attractions of Hereford and its neighbourhood, should be maintained in its present state, and this meeting feels that this end cannot be better secured than by appointing those who have hitherto managed it to resume their duties, and they therefore request the old committee, with the addition of the mayor and dean of Hereford, for the time being. To act as a committee for this purpose.[307]

Thus, the new *ad hoc* committee struggled on for another 18 years.

The Castle Green Trees

The vegetation on Castle Green went through a series of cycles. As the trees matured, the views from the upper walks were obscured, limbs began to drop and popular opinion began to call for their replacement. The original trees, most likely elms,

Fig. 76. The surviving elms on the Lower Walk, 1913.

were planted soon after 1753 – the accepted date for the establishment of the walks – and are depicted as a series of regular 'lollipops' on Taylor's plan of 1757. He also shows planting all round the Green with only the long terrace open. This seems to be mere conjecture on his part for Powle's view suggests that the north side of the Green, towards the Castle Pool, was still open in 1778 (Fig. 51). On the other hand, the *Beauties of England and Wales* (1805) notices the 'lower walk shaded by elms' but insists the trees were only found on the north and east where, perhaps, some new planting had taken place since 1778.[308] Wathen shows that within half a century the elms on the east side of the Green had reached maturity and might even have been developing some picturesque senility (Fig. 53). In the early 19th century veteran trees that displayed 'sudden varia-tions in form', as result of lightening strikes or tempests, were much admired, according to that connoisseur of ancient trees, Uvedale Price of Foxley.[309] However, as early as 1846, some of the elms had been condemned as dangerous and in 1858 young elms that had been growing in the parsonage at Weobley were transplanted onto the lower walk. Joseph Jones, writing in the late 1850s, noticed the change and commented that the 'lack of foliage permits the upper walk to command a considerable prospect'.[310] A further bout of planting took place in 1886 when three

Fig. 77. By the early 1920s only three mature elms had survived.

Fig. 78. A clump of mature elms on the bastion, 1918.

Sadly, in the same year two children were crushed by a falling elm, which inevitably led to a serious assault upon the surviving veterans. The postcards of this era show that the elms had been cleared from the eastern walk adjoining Mill Street, but at least four of the original trees, with fine straight trunks perhaps 20 to 25 feet in circumference, stood proudly along the lower walk (Figs. 76 & 77). Lime trees were the chosen replacement as they were regarded as more stable and less likely to break up in old age. They also had a particular kudos in late 19th century Herefordshire because of the philanthropic campaign to persuade the poor to keep bees, thus providing a cheap substitute for sugar.[312] Limes in England were pre-eminently the honey-tree and they had already been planted along the western edge of the Green, where there had previously been no trees, overlooking the private garden established on the site of the castle mount in Castle Hill. The dean and chapter were also at this date in the process of felling the elms surrounding the close and re-planting with limes.[313] By the First World War the picturesque qualities of Castle Green had been well and truly tamed. There had been much felling on the slopes of the ramparts overlooking Mill Street and the Castle Pool, leaving a single group of mature trees below the bastion at the south end of the Terrace to remind Edwardian promenaders of a less fastidious age of park improvement (Fig. 78). Fortunately, for today's visitors, the wild trees on the slopes were only coppiced and they have now joyfully recovered.

more elms were felled. On being sawn up, they were found to conceal lead bullets from the period of the Civil War – or so those with romantic inclinations conjectured. There were still those who revered the ancient trees and in 1894 Murray's *Handbook for Travellers* mentioned 'this spacious and healthy promenade formed by public subscription. The noble elms, twenty-one in number, are exhibiting symptoms of decay. They measure an average of twelve feet in circumference and were planted on the formation of the walks'.[311]

CHAPTER VII

Recreation : Under Council Management

The first Age of Council Ownership – 1873-1914

For 18 years the *ad hoc* committee of citizens ran Castle Green, securing subscriptions for its maintenance and the wages of the green keeper. Increasingly, the Green was used for public events, such as the summer show of the Hereford Horticultural Society, which was 'usually well attended'.[314] However, in 1873, as with previous attempts to support the Green from private funds, the committee ran into difficulties and once again the Green was rescued by the City Council. They obtained a lease from the county magistrates for 200 years at a peppercorn rent of £1 *per annum*. Taking the lead in the negotiations for the city was the owner of the *Hereford Times* and six times mayor, Alderman Charles Anthony, and the naturalist, Henry Graves Bull. Lords Bateman and Croft acted for the magistrates and insisted upon a number of awkward conditions, which took the city negotiators by surprise. In their turn, Messrs Anthony and Bull insisted that recent government legislation relating to 'people's parks' completely tied their hands in the matter and, furthermore, stated strongly that the magistrates had recently ignored their responsibilities to the Green 'leaving it to the management of a few private individuals without taking any interest in it'. Eventually, the City Council agreed to guarantee an annual expenditure of £20 upon the Green and to keep Mr. Dobbs, on as the green keeper, at 15s. per week.[315]

The Council took stock of their new responsibilities and gradually brought Castle Green into the top league of Edwardian municipal parks. One of its first tasks was to improve the area in Mill Street, where the mill pond had been temporarily filled up after 1863. This area had subsequently been annexed by the City Engineer, George Cole for his works department, before he moved in the early 1870s to purpose-built premises in Stonebow Road. A children's playground was then established here, but this annoyed the new residents of Mill Street and it was closed in 1887 and the site laid out as parkland with island beds. Trees were planted closely along the edge of Mill Street. When William Collins was writing in 1911 it was known as the 'lovers' lounge' suggesting that the vegetation, nourished by the deep silts of the moat, had produced sufficient cover for clandestine encounters.[316]

The Council had gradually acquired all the land to the north of the Castle Pool and in 1886 commenced the construction of Cantilupe Street. It is marked in outline on the 25 inch-to-a-mile Ordnance Survey plan of that year. Alfred Watkins remembered (1919) the city wall approaching Hogg's Mount, and photographed a stone-built summer-house erected on the broad-topped wall.[317] This appears to be marked on

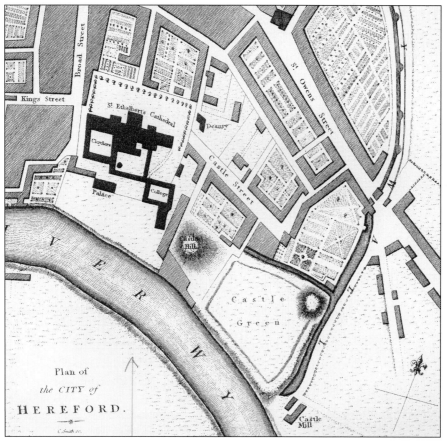

the plan accompanying Duncumb's *History* in 1804 and perhaps, as a detached building on Curley's plan of 1858 (Fig. 79). No doubt it was erected in the Georgian era by one of the genteel residents of Little Castle Street and had possibly been converted from the dovecote referred to in 1777.[318] The Council quickly colonised the area to the north of the Pool, cut off by the new street. Greenhouses were erected for propagation along the boundary wall of Castle Pool House and the 'exquisite flower beds' of the Cantilupe gardens were soon to follow. In 1904 a rustic bridge, constructed over the eastern end of the Castle Pool, linked the 'lovers lounge' in Mill Street with the new gardens. The bridge

Fig. 79. Plan from John Duncumb's Antiquities of the County of Hereford, Vol. I *(1804) – marking the summer house sited on the city wall below Hogg's Mount.*

Fig. 80. The Hereford Fire Brigade posing in front of the proposed Cantilupe Gardens, with pegs marking the position of the houses on the other side of the street (c.1883).

Fig. 81. A horse-drawn roller at work on the Green in 1908.

appears on the 1904 25 inch-to-a-mile Ordnance Survey plan and contemporary postcards. The wildfowl on the pool could look forward to a diet of stale bread for eternity! (Fig. 80).

Even in the hands of the Council the Green continued to be managed in the traditional way. The grass was still grazed by sheep (Fig. 37), which to late Victorian eyes, created an 'unsightly' appearance. However, a postcard of 1908 shows the first signs of mechanisation – a horse-drawn roller (Fig. 81). In 1882 Alderman E.E. Brosley became chairman of the Estates Committee and:

> began a series of reforms continued by his successors in office, so that today it is regarded as one of the beauty spots of Hereford – a combination of Old and New Hereford, of park and recreation ground, of lounge and promenade. It is the pride and admiration of the citizens of all ages.[319]

One of Alderman Brosley's first acts was to appoint a professional gardener as green keeper – Mr. John Wilson, who eventually opened a shop as a florist and seedsman in Commercial Street. Wilson, as Collins quaintly puts it, was 'a genuine lover and conservator of beautiful nature'. The postcards of the era provide a fitting testimonial to his efforts.

The area which particularly demanded attention was the site of the Castle Mill, which after its demolition in 1863 was rented as a private vegetable garden and orchard by Mr. A. Edwards. The General Hospital had annexed the site of the mill and enhanced the area in 1865 by building an ornamental lodge on the spoil heap.[320] However, the area down below, crossed by the path to Bartonsham, awaited improvement. Alfred Watkins, who remembered 'scrambling down the gully and over the ruined walls and foundations of Castle Mill', claimed that he was the leader of the citizens' agitation which led to the improvement of this area.[321] The path to Bartonsham was stabilised by the Council at a cost of £300 in 1893 and railings were added later after the death of three children who fell into the river whilst playing on the new steps beneath the path. The 'new garden and river walk' was opened by the mayor in July 1893 and some 10 years later was the subject of a special postcard, embossed in red with the city's arms (Fig. 82).[322] This showed the garden newly planted with shrub roses and enclosed by a new, wrought iron fence with intersecting arches. There were plenty of benches, a new gas lamp and a fence with a rustic herringbone pattern next to the river. At the far end, where the path set off for Bartonsham, there was a rustic cottage for the proprietoress of the *Princess Mary* ferryboat. Collins admired this 'riverside alcove with its inviting and retiring lounges' (Pl. 7). Within four years the Victoria Bridge was constructed to connect this new garden with the Bishop's Meadows (Fig. 83). This Diamond Jubilee Memorial 'artistic in design, picturesque in appearance, elegant in form, light in construction, beautiful in effect and altogether worthy of the traditions of an ancient city', was paid for by public subscription and designed by the City Engineer, John Parker (Pl. 8)

ARMS OF HEREFORD

Fig. 82. A special postcard issued to commemorate the 1893 opening of the new 'alcove' gardens beneath the Infirmary wall. The card is 1903 or later (info. Tim Ward)

*Fig. 83. Bowling on the Green before the creation of an enclosure (*c.*1908).*

Fig. 84. Jubilee celebrations, Hogg's Mount, 1897.

Fig. 85. Maypole dancing at the coronation of Edward VII in 1911.
(Derek Foxton collection)

Hereford's citizens were so enamoured. Alfred Watkins for one regretted the dividing up of the only large public space in Hereford. He remembered how it had been used for Queen Victoria's Jubilee celebrations in June 1897 when almost 900 people attended an evening concert of patriotic songs. On this occasion Hogg's Mount acted as a grandstand, rising above the amphitheatre of the Green (Fig. 84). A similar festival, involving the recently-founded Boy Scouts and Girl Guides demonstrating their skills at maypole dancing, occurred in 1911 to celebrate the coronation of Edward VII (Fig. 85). A little earlier, in September 1908 the Green was used by Messrs. Heins & Co. for a 'gramophone concert', whilst in 1914, on the eve of the First World War, the Herefordshire Volunteers mustered here (Fig. 86).[323]

The spacious extent of the Green was somewhat compromised in 1908 by the mayor's resolution to hand over a small area to form a permanent bowling green. Earlier post-cards show that bowling was already taking place in an informal manner, but the new green was run by a Bowling Green Committee which paid the Council a generous rent, utilised for improvements elsewhere in the park. Bowling was open to all, to encourage healthy recreation (Pl. 10), but not all

Fig. 86. A muster of the Herefordshire Volunteers on Castle Green in 1914.
(Derek Foxton collection)

The Ornamental Planting[324]

One of the major differences between the municipal park and what had gone before was the
appearance of a great deal of fencing. John
Wilson clearly convinced the Council that if the
Green was to follow the example of the 'people's
parks', which were appearing in every large town
in England at this time, the public had to be carefully managed and shunted along well-defined
routes.[325] The picturesque with its romantic,
natural and accessible scenery was about to give
way to High Victorian formality – bedding, flowering shrubberies and artificial settings for
viewing. The entire green was surrounded with
iron or concrete posts with wire strands and chain
link swags – well displayed on a winter postcard
of the period (Fig. 76). In practical terms this kept
the grazing sheep off the new tarmacadam paths,
but it also restricted the use of the grass. As it was
only three feet high, the energetic could step over
it. Around the new planting areas, iron fencing,
prettily designed with interweaving arches and

two horizontal bars, was employed. This fence
provided an impenetrable barrier for footballs,
boys and all but the smallest of dogs. Within
these enclosures, generally placed at the junction
of paths where they could be admired, ornamental gardening could safely take place.

On entering the Green along St. Ethelbert's
Lane, there was a bed, as there is today opposite
The Fosse, which appears on some postcards
planted with ferns and ivies, on others, rather
neglected (Fig. 87). Clearly, the age of formal
bedding arrived late at this spot. Where the upper
and lower walks set off towards Hogg's Mount,
there was a border with low bedding, enclosed by
fencing between the two paths. Opposite, on the
corner of the Green, there was a low shrubbery,
presumably sited in part to discourage visitors
from wearing an informal path onto the Green
(Pl. 11). Further along the lower walk there was
another bed occupying the slope between the upper
and lower walks. This seems to have been relatively
short-lived, but on a postcard dated 1913 it looks

intensive, with a gardener bent over his work. All the way along the upper walk, the wilderness above the Castle Pool had been tamed and behind the link fence there were flowering shrubs, holly balls and, in 1913, newly planted standard trees. It is noticeable that, throughout the park, new trees, prominently placed, are provided with elegant metal tree guards with splayed tops. The slopes of Castle Cliff also seem to have been brought well under control. The tree cover was kept low, until it reached the south bastion where some tall elms sprouted from the lower level. Watkins took a photograph looking along here in *c*.1920 with the May blossom providing a striking show (Fig. 88; Pl. 12). The hedge along the Terrace was no higher than the fence – about three feet – and in the years before the First World War large yuccas were planted just beyond the hedge (Fig. 78). From their consistent positions on a series of

Fig. 87. View along Castle Pool before the advent of formal bedding (c.1900).

Fig. 88. View of the cliff terrace – Alfred Watkins c.1920.

cards it appears they survived in this position during successive winters.

Where the terrace path turned the corner beside the bastion, there were enclosed beds on either side of the path, just before the steps that led down to the new gardens by the Victoria Bridge (Fig. 89). On the Green side of the path there was a mixed border with herbaceous plants and shrubs, whilst on the south-east side cards indicate that there were standard roses under-planted with

bedding and permanent ground cover. Two cards of *c*. 1920 show a small but prominent tiered tree, perhaps a *Cornus controversa*. Some time before the War, the steps down to the bridge were enclosed with rustic fencing with a herringbone pattern. The bank was revetted with clinker, as it is today, and was planted informally, with the addition of several small standard trees. Postcards indicate that the rose garden in the 'riverside alcove', established in 1893, was relatively short-lived and

Fig. 89. The corner bed beside the bastion – bedding protected by fencing (c.1920).

in 1918 was planted with shrubs – a result, perhaps, of the shortage of labour during the War (Pl. 13).

Nelson's column, surrounded by its seven guns and a high iron fence became increasingly shrubby in the late 19th century. Its pedestal was covered in ivy, carefully clipped around the inscription tablet (Fig. 90). The improvement below the Infirmary in 1893 led to a regular correspondence in the *Hereford Times* about improving the setting of the column. Particular criticism was levelled at the 'heavy yews and boxes' cut into 'plum pudding shapes' at the base of the column – the vestiges of the picturesque planting put in earlier in the century. The writers wanted carpet bedding and the removal of the heavy fencing. In addition, the guns could be provided with a new home on Hogg's Mount. The editor of the paper added that if the use of sheep on the Green was terminated and some 'other methods of keeping down the grass investigated', the railings around the column could be removed completely.[326] Other postcards indicate that the spirit of this idea was implemented, just in time it seems for the Trafalgar celebrations of 1905, when the column was decorated with garlands (Fig. 91). The

Fig. 90. Nelson's column with neatly clipped ivy, high railings and guns (c.1900).

Fig. 91. Nelson's column decorated for Trafalgar Day celebrations, 1905.

shrubs soon disappeared and a formal bedding scheme appeared, generally edged with white – probably annual alyssum – and much appreciated by the postcard photographers who produced many images during this period. As the detail seems to change on each postcard, the gardening staff clearly used this bed to display their inventiveness and skill. Four of the cannons remained for a time, but the high fencing was replaced with low chain-links, suggesting that the mechanical mower had replaced the sheep sometime before 1914 (Pl. 14).

The early 20th century: 1914-45

William Collins, writing one of his last books on his beloved city in the midst of 'the terrible war', found in Castle Green a catalyst for his nostalgia. (Pl. 15). 'At midday, when the landscape is bathed with floods of brilliant radiance, and at eventide, when the declining sun fills the glowing west with gorgeous beauty, our minds are taken back in time "when inspiration hover'd o'er the ground"'. Its 'great charm' he pondered was to be found in its 'brotherhood of venerable tall elms, centuries old, and sylvan shade' which casts a 'quiet reposeful and sweet spell'. Alfred Watkins, writing a decade later, remembered fondly the festivals and celebrations of Edwardian days and asserted that the Green was no longer used for public occasions. In part, he thought this was the result of earlier improvements – bedding, fencing and the enclosure of the bowling green and Nelson's column – which had reduced the useful public space. Without articulating it as such he yearned for the informality of the picturesque park.[327]

Fig. 92. Interwar solitude – Castle Green in the 1930s.

The postcards of the era certainly indicate that the Green was a place of quiet recreation and rarely do the images contain more than one or two people. Indeed, the solitary mother with a child and small groups of placid children appear to be the essential props used by the professional photographer on his visit to Hereford (Fig. 92). Many of the Edwardian photographs were reprinted year after

Fig. 93. The timber bandstand used for social and political purposes in the 1940s.
(Derek Foxton collection)

year, and the date indicated by the postmark is often a poor guide to the date of the image. Thus, postcards become less valuable as a source of historical information, creating a visual hiatus in the 1920s before the advent of the cheap camera.

The one event which figures consistently in the calendar for Castle Green in the early 20th century is Empire Day, which celebrated Queen Victoria's birthday on 24 May and, after 1918, was diligently observed as a school holiday. Like the modern May Bank Holiday it was celebrated as the beginning of the summer and thus inaugurated the 'season' for outdoor pursuits. It was at this time of year that Mr. Gwilliam opened the kiosk which had arrived at the southern end of the upper walk in 1922. It was a sign of the times that it was not open on Sundays, but adjoining it there was a tea garden – that essential destination for day-trippers between the wars.[328]

At some point in the 1920s the kiosk was joined by another permanent structure, rather late in arrival – the bandstand. This was a wooden rectangular construction – much like a contemporary 'motor house' – under a gabled roof. It was open all round, with the front enclosed with a slatted balustrade. Adjoining it was a small shed where seats could be stored (Fig. 93). There can be no doubt that it revived the social life of Castle Green after the Great War and during the 1930s it was especially favoured as a venue for band concerts and choral performances. In the summer of 1932, for example, the Pontypool Wesley Male Voice Choir booked it for Whit Monday and at regular intervals throughout the summer the Herefordshire YMCA Orchestra, accompanied by the Elite Singers, gave free concerts. A 'dancing enclosure', presumably with a floor, was also available and this was hired by the *Daily Express* in July for a community concert as part of its campaign to cheer up the country during the depression. For the same reason, no doubt, the City Council experimented with weekly concerts and dancing throughout the summer of 1930. However, in July, they were cancelled through lack of support and the Estates Committee had their knuckles rapped. As a result, the newly-established Development Committee – in charge of promoting the city in the new age of mass tourism – took over arranging events on the Green.

The bandstand was well used during the Second World War and the Hereford Recreation Society provided a piano to accompany soloists, whilst in 1944 electricity was supplied, making it an ideal venue for political and community meetings which required a public address system. The building was repainted in the same year and repaired again in 1951. It was taken away sometime before 1967 when a new concrete bandstand was erected in the recently landscaped Redcliffe Gardens (the site of the castle motte), which in turn, was demolished in the early 1990s.

The original bandstand was joined by another timber building – the Bowling Club Pavilion – in

1933. This was paid for out of the Jackson Bequest, a windfall of £7,000 given to the city in 1930 to enhance social provision. It initiated a vigorous debate and throughout the early '30s various schemes were proposed, including a paddling pool for children which was to be excavated on the site of the flowerbed below the hospital wall. This was the first of many child-centred initiatives during this era which, if they had all come to fruition, would have seri-ously damaged the land-

Fig. 94. Early 20th century view of the Science and Art School, showing the Regency pavilion.

scape qualities of the Green. Eventually, in July 1932, it was decided that £1,250 of the Jackson Bequest was to be set aside to erect a 'Bowling Green Shelter'. This was designed by the City Surveyor, Neil Shimmin, and constructed as a sectional building by Ellis & Co. of Hackney. A charming watercolour elevation was presented to the Estates Committee in February 1933 (Pls. 16, 17). It shows a rather delicate building under a sweeping, rather chinoiserie roof with a central door beyond a balcony. There were windows on both sides and a central gable with a clock, provided by the Chairman of the Estates Committee, Mrs. Louise Luard. The building exists today, but has lost all its ornamental quality in endeavouring to keep the vandals at bay.

The principal building of quality on the Green remained the Regency temple at the south-eastern end of Castle Cliffe House. It added considerable dignity to the pleasure grounds and was present on virtually every postcard of the early 20th century (Fig. 94). The old museum and baths had been taken over by the School of Art, soon after the opening of the Free Library and Museum in Broad Street in 1874. Apparently, there was also a Science and Art School that occupied the class-rooms provided in the new Library, but by 1900

this appears to have amalgamated with the insti-tution on Castle Green, which was now called the Science and Art School. It was an independent institution, run by a 'master' and assisted by a secretary/treasurer. At some point in the 1920s the School was brought under the control of the Herefordshire Education Committee and from then the Director of Education is listed in the *Directories* as the secretary/treasurer. This change was reflected in the destruction of the temple, the upkeep of which had become the responsibility of the County Council. In 1932 the City Council Minutes noticed the removal of the 'Art School porch' (presumably an illiterate refer-ence to the pediment) and the creation of a new entrance to the College 'round the corner'.[329] This is shown in postcards of the period, which show the portico minus the pediment (Fig. 95). At some point after the Second World War, perhaps during the early '60s just before the College moved to its new premises in Folly Lane, the portico was under-built. The wall and its windows were brought forward and the freestanding columns converted into pilasters. Other utilitarian addi-tions were added to the building, defacing and confusing the original composition. Thus, Castle Green lost its principal monument (after Nelson's

*Fig. 95. The mutilated pavilion with an upper storey added
and with the arcade filled in (c.1955).*

column), which had existed in one form or another since the mid –18th century.

The economic depression of the '30s posed a serious threat to the well-manicured and labour-intensive public pleasure grounds. In 1930-31 the government was on the one hand urging local authorities to make economies but, on the other, was keen to encourage employment. Whilst a scheme was being considered to use the out-of-work to level the Bishop's Meadows, each department of the Council was being urged to reduce expenditure. The Estates Committee, with an annual budget of between £100 and £200, managed to save £30 in 1931 by cancelling Sunday work and reducing expenditure on plants. The labour intensive flower bed beneath the hospital wall was reduced in size and the Rotary Club took on the task of tidying up the nearby riverside beach, which in the summer was much used by children and bathers.

Remarkably, the cuts brought some unexpected benefits as the great and the good of the city and county began making gifts to maintain the beauty and interest of the park. In December 1930 Mrs. Luard set an example by providing 40 lbs. of daffodil bulbs to be planted on the slopes of the Green overlooking the Castle Pool. The following year, Mr. R.O. Backhouse of Sutton Court, the famous daffodil breeder, provided 1,250 bulbs to be planted on the Green.[330] He was soon joined by Sid Wright, a local businessman, Mrs. Feltham, the mayor's wife, and many members of the local squirarchy. Soon herbaceous plants and roses were being provided, including a 'very large gift of choice chrysanthemums' from the superintendent of Regent's Park, London. Even more welcome, was the gift of water fowl, including a pair of mandarin ducks, given by Mrs. Astley of Brinsop Court, to be released on the Castle Pool. They were obviously an attraction and were soon joined by a pair of shelducks, provided by Councillor Symonds. Unfortunately, they either died or took flight as, soon after, the Town Clerk was instructed to find a source of shelduck eggs. He was unsuccessful, but the Lord Chamberlain offered a royal swan. This was welcomed by the Estates Committee who, between the members, shared the cost of catching the bird, packaging and carriage. In December 1931 the swan was to be seen on the

Pool, gliding over the recently introduced trout, again provided by a member of the public – Captain Pritchard.

This remarkable outburst of civic pride and philanthropy ensured that Castle Green retained its reputation and affection amongst the people of Hereford during a period of austerity. Notwithstanding the failure of the monthly concerts, there was a great deal taking place on the Green, which helped to distract the citizens from the economic problems and the developing international crisis. One of the high points of the summer in the 1930s was the flower show organised by the West of England Rose Society each July. The Green was full of exhibition stalls and attendance was so high that special 'sleepers' were put down to protect the grass and paths in wet weather. Only the bowling green was out of bounds. A putting tournament was also held in August 1931 and the following year the annual carnival assembled there. Various national organisations held

rallies on the Green, such as the Red Cross, the British Legion and, more picturesquely, the English Folk Dance Society – all in 1934. The usage of the Green was so intense that when the Woolhope Club asked if it could carry out an excavation there in May 1934, its request was refused. Eventually, after some behind the scenes lobbying, permission was granted for a ten-day excavation from 1 October. Sadly, the proposed director, Alfred Watkins, was ill and the secretary of the Club, George Marshall, wrote to ask for a postponement.[331]

During this time Castle Green appears to have had a resident green keeper. His Regency house, near the Fosse, survived until *c*.1940, and maybe a little beyond (Figs. 96 & 97). His responsibilities increased during this period, with the addition of the Bishop's Meadow and the Edgar Street 'Athletic Ground' to the stock of public amenity land. To make regular visits to his expanding empire in 1934, the Estates Committee set aside £6 to provide him with a bicycle. He also enjoyed the use of a punt on the Castle Pool provided by Mr. J. Jordan in 1934. The focus for gardening activity on the Green was at the rear of the Cantilupe gardens where, as a postcard of the period indicates, there were at least three greenhouses and

Left: Fig. 96. The Nelson memorial and the green keeper's house about 1900.

Above: Fig 97. The green keeper's house.

miscellaneous frames and huts. The card also shows the punt and royal swans (Pl. 18). The proximity of the propagation houses meant that the Cantilupe gardens received much attention and were used throughout this period to display the arts of the municipal gardener with much bedding-out and carefully pruned 'lollipop' roses. Even at the height of the depression the Council paid for several extra seats to be placed there. With its long frontage on the Pool, bosky back-drop – enhanced by daffodils in season – it was already a favourite spot for the elderly and parents with young children.

The later 20th century:
1945 to the present day

Castle Green emerged after the Second World War virtually unscathed. Its iron fencing survived in the main, although there was some looped fencing purchased by the Council in 1953. Land near Hogg's Mount had been used for ammuni-tion shelters during the war, presumably as part of the dispersal policy for munitions made at Rotherwas. They were moved by the War Department in December 1945. The School of Art was obviously expanding and the Education Committee tried to convince the Estates Committee that the erection of temporary build-

ings, perhaps on the shelter site, would not adversely damage the Green. Fortunately, the Committee thought otherwise and the College simply got a new cycle rack.

Towards the end of the war the City Council began negotiating with three landowners in possession of property in Castle Hill.[332] Remarkably, considering the Council's consci-entiousness in asserting its ownership of the Barbican and Castle Hill in the 18th century, in the next century the property quietly slipped out of their hands and the original tenancies became three freeholds of garden ground. The largest area – 3,388 square yards – occupied the site of the mount, and in 1945 belonged to Mrs. Steel of 29 Castle Street. The Council offered her £500. A lane to the east of Mrs. Steel's holding separated it from the other two gardens, which formed a narrow strip of land backing up against the Green Keeper's house. The more southerly garden, of 823 square yards, belonged to Miss Victor, whose enjoyment of her property was inconvenienced by the presence of a 'urinal' perched above her on the western edge of the Green. This infamous loo seems to have arrived in the late 19th century and is marked on the 25inch Ordnance Survey plan of 1904. Naturally, the Edwardian postcards draw a leafy veil over its presence, but in June 1934 the Estates Committee decided to replace the 'conve-niences' (ladies too?) with 'more modern structures'. History does not record Miss Victor's response, but when the Girl Guides held a rally on the Green in May 1948, they were given permission to use the Arts School facilities. The small rect-angular garden, which had once been attached to the Green Keeper's Lodge, which was 630 square yards in extent, in 1946 belonged to Miss K.R. Evelyn. Both these ladies are absent from the contemporary *Directories* and were presumably absentee

Fig. 98. The cider press from Breinton House – erected near the bastion in 1949.

landowners who rented their gardens to lesser folk. The Lodge itself, last photographed in 1947, belonged to T.A. Matthews, a solicitor and estate agent, and was presumably demolished soon after this date. The entire property was secured by the Council around 1948.

The Council used their new acquisition to establish a nursery. The free-standing greenhouse in the Cantilupe gardens, together with the gardener's mess hut and cold frames, were moved to the new site.

Fig. 99. *Modern movement cascade and bandstand, illustrated in 1969.*

The lean-to greenhouse was demolished and the Cantilupe gardens extended. The old summer house was replaced and a little later, in 1951, the 'bridge' over the eastern end of the Castle Pool was repaired. A new greenhouse (25 feet by 12 feet), designed by the City Surveyor's department, was provided by Messrs. Messenger & Co. of Loughborough in 1950 at a cost of £381. Harding Bros. of Commercial Street supplied the heating system and at the same time put radiators in the mess hut. The new greenhouse was to be kept at a high temperature and was tall enough for large palms.

There were several other significant proposals and innovations in this period. The bowling green had been neglected during the war and the turf had developed bald areas. In addition, the watering facilities were inadequate. After some debate, the Council provided £1,008 in 1949 enabling Bradshaw Bros. of Leicester to relay the green with the best Lancashire sea-washed turf. In the same year, Lord Chesterfield (originally of Holme Lacy House) offered a cider mill to the city, if it was removed at the Council's expense from Breinton House. The surveyor, Walter Shimmin, got his assistant Ken Lee, 'being of an artistic nature', to make a sketch for the Council showing the arrangement of the press at the south-eastern ern end of the Terrace where the cannons first appeared in the late 18th century. The Council was charmed and the press was erected, with the addition of a new flowerbed (Fig. 98), but it was moved again in the 1960s. There was a drinking fountain on the Green, perhaps close to the loos, which began to give trouble in 1950 and was subsequently renewed. To make the park more child friendly, there was a proposal in 1947 to erect a roundabout on the Green. This came to nothing, but a similar aspiration moved the surveyor to invite a group of students from the Welsh School of Architecture to design a lido for Castle Green. Again nothing followed, but in a sense these schemes were eventually realised on the Bishop's Meadow in the early 1970s. Once again, Castle Green had a narrow escape.

During the early 1960s the nursery was once again relocated on the old Sanitary Laundry site off Ledbury Road. Thus, the Redcliffe Gardens, financed by a private bequest and money from the Herefordshire Development Association, were laid out by the Surveyor, Graham Roberts. The modernist design in concrete, with a cascade, ornamental bridge and pool, was accompanied by

Fig. 100. Castle Cliffe – a picturesque wilderness succumbing to 'grasscrete' in 1973.

a new bandstand with a cantilevered roof. Conceived at the end of an era of brass bands and tea-time quartets, its position in a residential suburb became untenable with the advent of amplifiers and modern pop. Its creator claims it was removed because of 'vandalism ... and a lack of resources'.[333] Time would, perhaps, have made it better appreciated and the illustration of it in the *Hereford: Official Guide* (1969) in the year of its creation, suggests that the city may have lost a minor work of art – a bold statement for its time (Fig. 99). The loos were also replaced with 'more modern structures', and in 1967-8 the Victoria Footbridge was reconditioned at a cost of £12,000, which was ten times its original price in 1897. In 1969 the Art College moved to its new premises in Folly Lane and the old museum building was occupied by the Technical College, whilst the baths beneath were refurbished as a canoe centre.

Having consolidated the riverside and constructed some new steps for the canoe centre, the Council decided to stabilise Castle Cliff. The vegetation, including a mature Holm oak (*Quercus ilex*), was cleared from the bank and heavy equipment employed to grade the surface ready for the laying of 'grasscrete' – concrete blocks with apertures for grass to grow, frequently used for car parks (Fig. 101). In one blow the natural accretions of centuries – including many ancient burials – were destroyed. There was a great outcry with representations from individuals, local and national societies, news coverage in the *Telegraph* and on BBC television. The Council met representatives of the protesters and some attempt was made to ameliorate the damage.[334] The bank was to be planted with mature trees and wild flower seeds were to be scattered in the new soil spread over the concrete. A 'sea-side' like promenade along the base of the cliff was abandoned, but the harsh new retaining wall, built out of randomly coursed Forest of Dean stone, was constructed, as was the bijou bastion at the south-eastern end of the Terrace (modelled on the feature displayed on Taylor's plan). It contained the equipment necessary to raise water from the river to feed the ailing Castle Pool.

In the long term the Castle Cliff saga had some beneficial results. It initiated some exciting archaeology on the southern tip of the Green, which took the history of the site deep into the Dark Ages. It also saw the foundation of Hereford's first amenity society – the Hereford Civic Trust (latterly, Society) – and it was an important landmark in developing public awareness of the significance of the Castle Green landscape. The wild cliff, it was realised, was an important link with the picturesque of the 18th century. Today the Cliff and the Green once again suffers, this time more from neglect rather than thoughtless innovation, but the future looks brighter with the formation in 2003 of the Friends of Castle Green and a possible National Lottery application to restore the Green to its Edwardian climax.

References

Abbreviations

BAR – British Archaeological Reports
Cal. Inq. Misc. – Calendar of Inquisitions Miscellaneous
Cal. Misc. – Calendar of Miscellaneous Rolls
Cal. Pat. – Calendar of Patent Rolls
Cal. State Papers Dom. Calendar of Domestic State Papers
Cath. Muns. – Cathedral Muniments
CBA – Council for British Archaeology
Hist. MSS. Comm. – Historical Manuscripts Commission
HAN – Herefordshire Archaeological News
HCA – Hereford Cathedral Archives
HCL – Hereford City Library
HRO – Hereford Record Office
HJ – Hereford Journal
HT – Herefore Times
PR – Pipe Rolls
TBGAS – Transactions of the Bristol and Gloucester Archaeological Society
TWNFC – Transactions of the Woolhope Naturalists Field Club

1. T.S. Aldis, 'Drift in the Wye Valley' in *TWNFC* (1904), 327.
2. H.C. Moore, 'Drifts in Herefordshire' in *TWNFC* (1904), 331-3.
3. *TWNFC* (1961), 373, 393.
4. *TWNFC* (1931), 127.
5. Oliver Rackham, *Trees and Woodlands in the British Landscape* (1993), 27-8.
6. F.G. Heys & J.F.L. Norwood, 'Excavations on the supposed line of King's Ditch' in *TWNFC* (1958), 122.
7. A.T. Bannister, *The Cathedral Church of Hereford* (1924), 113.
8. T. Curley, 'A Local deposit of Peat at Hereford' in *TWNFC* (1866), 253-4.
9. R. Shoesmith, *Hereford Excavations* 3 (CBA Research Report 53, 1985), 21; A. Thomas & A. Boucher (eds.), *Hereford City Excavations* 4 (2002), 149-50.
10. *Ibid.,* Shoesmith, 90; S.C. Stanford, *The Archaeology of the Welsh Marches* (1980), 108.
11. *TWNFC* (2002), 388; Richard Stone & Nic Appleton-Fox, *A View from Hereford's Past* (1996), 62.
12. R. Shoesmith, *Hereford City Excavations* 2 (CBA Report 46, 1982), 29-31.
13. J. Tonkin, 'Early Street Names of Hereford' in *TWNFC* (1966), 246, 248; Victor Watts (ed.), *Cambridge Dictionary of English Place-Names* (2004), 473-4, 509.
14. William Capes, *Charters and Records of Hereford Cathedral* (1908), 88.
15. John Blair, *The Church in Anglo-Saxon Society* (2005), 288-9.
16. M. Costen, *The Origins of Somerset* (1992), 56-73.
17. John Lloyd, *A History of Wales* I (1939), 281-2; *Iolo MSS* (1848), 86.
18. H.P.R. Finberg, *Lucerna* (1964), 72.
19. Wendy Davies, *An Early Welsh Microcosm* (1978), 65-107.
20. P. Sims-Williams, *Religion and Literature in Western England 600-800* (1990), 77; Blair, *Anglo-Saxon Society,* 28, 31, 62-3.
21. Bruce Coplestone-Crow, *Herefordshire Place-Names* (BAR 214, 1989), 11-13.
22. Margaret Gelling, *Signposts to the Past* (1978), 102-5.
23. O. S. Anderson, *English Hundred-Names* (1934), 165-6.

24. P. Rahtz & P. Fowler, 'Somerset A.D. 400-700' in P. Fowler (ed.), *Archaeology and the Landscape* (1972), 194-8; L. Alcock, 'The activities of potentates in Celtic Britain A.D. 500-800' in S.C. Driscoll & M.R. Niek (eds.), *Power and Politics in Early Medieval Britain and Ireland* (1988), 22-39; Kate Pretty, 'Defining the Magonsaete' in Steven Bassett (ed.), *The Origins of Anglo-Saxon Kingdoms* (1989), 178-9.

25. Helen Cam, *Liberties and Commumities in Medieval England*, (1944), 64,87-8, 105; Della Hooke, *The Anglo-Saxon Landscape*, (1985), 75-8, 94-9.

26. Keith Ray, 'Archaeology and the Early Church of Herefordshire' in Ann Malpas (ed.), *The Early Church in Herefordshire* (2001), 175-6; S.C. Stanford, *Welsh Marches*, 176, but see Coplestone-Crow, *Herefordshire Place-Names*, 108.

27. S.H. Martin, 'The Chapel of St Dubric in Woolhope' in *TWNFC* (1954), 229-32; *The Valor Ecclesiasticus* III (1817), 34; *Registrum Ade de Orleton* (Canterbury and York Society, 1908), 386.

28. Pretty, Defining the Magonsaete, 182-3; Barbara Yorke, *Kings and Kingdoms in Early Anglo-Saxon England* (1990), 107-8.

29. Frank & Caroline Thorn (eds.), *Domesday Book: Herefordshire* (1983), 6.3, 7.5, 29.3; HRO, St Guthlac's Cartulary (microfilm), 381, 384 –6.

30. *Cal. Pat. 1321-4,* 49; Bannister, *Cathedral Church*, 20-4.

31. Julia Barrow, *English Episcopal Acta VII: Hereford 1079-1234* (1993), 22.87.

32. Sims-Williams, *Religion and Literature*, 88-91.

33. Joe Hillaby, 'The Early Church in Herefordshire : Columban or Roman?' in Malpas, *Early Church in Herefordshire*, 41-59.

34. A. Morly & C.N.L. Brooke (eds.), *The Letters and Charters of Gilbert Foliot* (1967), 300.

35. *Registrum Johannis Trefnant* (Canterbury and York Society, 1914), 164-7.

36. Della Hooke, *The Anglo-Saxon Landscape*, 15; Sims-Williams, *Religion and Literature*, 41-2, 90-91.

37. *Ibid.*, 138-9; For Inkberrow see P.H. Sawyer, *Anglo-Saxon Charters* (1968), 1430, 1432, 1460.

38. J.G. Evans, *The Text of the Book of Llan Dav* (1893), 192; Rev. J. Williams (ed.), *Annales Cambriae* (Rolls Series, 1860), 10-11; T. Jones (ed.), *Brut y Tywysogyon* (1952), 2. See also Joe Hillaby in Malpas, *Early Church in Herefordshire*, 58 who considers that the dispersed nature of the cathedral estates suggests a late and piecemeal process of endowment.

39. J. Duncumb, *History and Antiquities of the County of Hereford* I (1804), 522; Shoesmith, *Hereford Excavations* 2, 76-77; Blair, *Church in Society*, 287.

40. R. Shoesmith, *Hereford City Excavations* 1, (CBA Report 36, 1980), 48-56;.Blair, *Church in Society*, 287.

41. David Whitehead, 'In Search of St Ethebert's Well' *HAN* (1978), 11-13; Blair, *Church in Society*, 196-8, 223; Davies, *Microcosm*, 37-8.

42. M.R. James, 'Two Lives of St Ethelbert, King and Martyr' in *Eng. Hist. Rev.* 32 (1917), 214-44.

43. B. Colgrave (ed.), *Felix, Life of St Guthlac* (1956), 1-10; H. Mayr-Harting, 'Guthlac' in *DNB* (2004-6); Joe & Caroline Hillaby, *Leominster Minster*, (2006), 136.

44. Alan Thacker, 'Kings, Saints and Monasteries in Pre-Viking Mercia' in *Midland History* 10 (1985), 5-6.

45. Tim Hoverd speaking at the Castle Green Lectures in October 2005. Reports on Ashgrove are in *TWNFC* (1943), cvi and (1949), xvi-xvii, as well as *HAN* 65 (1996), 32. Another 'Saxon' graveyard at Sutton was reported in the *Hereford Journal* 22 August 1798 at 'the top of Sutton Upper Field' and was said to contain 'part of King Offa's army'!

46. Summarised in Keith Ray & Tim Hoverd, *Archaeologcal Work at Sutton St Michael, Herefordshire 1999: An Interim Statement* (2000).

47. Blair, *Church in Society*, 287-9.

48. *Ibid.,* 280-85; J. Blair, 'The Anglo-Saxon Church in Herefordshire' in Malpas, *Early Church*, 5-7.

49. John H. Williams, Michael Shaw & Varian Denham, *Middle Saxon Palaces at Northampton* (1985), 37-42.

50. St Peter was the favourite dedication of King Offa – Sims-Williams, *Religion and Literature*, 161-4.

51. D.C. Douglas & G. Greenaway, *English Historical Documents* II (1968), 897-8.

52. The parish boundaries are conveniently presented in M.D. Lobel, *Historic Towns: Hereford* (1968).

53. J.N. Dalton, *The Manuscriptes of St George's Chapel, Windsor Castle* (1957), 275; *The Valor Ecclesiasticus* III (1810-35), 27.

54. S.H. Martin, 'St Guthlac's Priory and the City Churches' in *TWNFC* (1954), 219-222.

55. W.H. Hart (ed.), *Historia Cartularium Monasterii Sancti Petri Gloucestriae* I (Rolls Series, 1863), 329.

56. J.E.B. Gover, A. Mawer & F.M. Stenton, *The Place-Names of Northamptonshire* (1933), xvii-xviii.

57. Hillaby in Malpas, *Early Church in Herefordshire*, 58; Barrow, *Episcopal Acta*, 21, 22, 27, 87, 125, 155, 204.

58. S.R. Bassett, 'Churches in Worcester before and after the conversion of the Anglo-Saxons' in *Antiquaries Journal* 69 (1989), 225-56; Steven Bassett, 'Anglo-Saxon Shrewsbury and its churches' in *Midland History* 16 (1991), 1-24.

59. Lobel, *Historic Towns*, 2 & plan based upon the constituency boundaries of the early 19th century: Jakeman & Carver, *Hereford Directory* (1902), 309.

60. James, 'Two Lives of St Ethelbert', 242; John Webb (ed.), 'A Roll of the Household Expenses of Richard de Swinfield, bishop of Hereford during part of the years 1289-90' in *Camden Society* I (1855), xix.

61. B.G. Charles & H.D. Emmanuel (eds.), *Calendar of the earlier Hereford Cathedral Muniments* II (1955), No.740- dated 1312.

62. See note 55.

63. Carolyn Heighway, 'Saxon Gloucester' in J. Haslam, *Anglo-Saxon Towns* (1984), 360-1.

64. Nicholas Brooks & Catherine Cubitt (eds.), *St Oswald of Worcester* (1996), 143-4; David Whitehead, *The Book of Worcester* (1976), 87-8; E. Klingelhofer, 'Evidence of Town Planning in Late Saxon Warwick' in *Midland History* III (1975), 2; Williams, *Middle Saxon Palaces*, 6-7.
65. Blair, *Church and Society*, 365.
66. F.M. Stenton, *Anglo-Saxon England* (1971), 230-8, 252-61.
67. G.N. Garmonsway (ed.), *Anglo-Saxon Chronicle* (1953), 87.
68. Don Stansbury, *The Lady who fought the Vikings* (1993), 109-69.
69. Shoesmith, *Hereford Excavations* 2, 77-82.
70. Blair, *Church and Society*, 223-35.
71. F.T. Wainwright, 'Aethelflaed, Lady of the Mercians' in Peter Clemoes (ed.), *The Anglo –Saxons* (1959), 66-7; Garmonsway, *Anglo-Saxon Chronicle*, 97-100; William of Malmsbury, *Gesta Regnum* I (Rolls Series, 1887-9), 148; M. Hare, 'Kings, Crowns and Festivals' in *TBGAS,* CXV (1997), 41-78; Thorn, *Herefordshire Domesday*, C.3, 1.3, 1.4, 35; H.M. Colvin, *History of the King's Works*, I (1963), 27
72. Hillaby in Malpas, *Early Church in Herefordshire*, 58-9, quoting A.M. Pearn, 'The Origin and Development of Urban Churches and Parishes: A Comparative Study of Hereford, Shrewsbury and Chester' unpublished Cambrideg Ph.D. thesis (1989).
73. Garmonsway, *Anglo-Saxon Chronicle*, 101-4.
74. Heighway in Haslam, *Anglo-Saxon Towns*, 371-2.
75. Bassett, 'Anglo-Saxon Shrewsbury', 9-10.
76. D. Whitelock (ed.), *Anglo-Saxon Wills* (1930), 54-6; Robertson, *Anglo-Saxon Charters*, 186.
77. Lobel, *Historic Towns*, 2-3.
78. Joe Hillaby, 'The Norman New Town of Hereford' in *TWNFC* (1983), 181-95.
79. Charles & Emmanuel, *Cathedral Muniments*, III, 1095; Capes, *Charters and Records*, xxxii, 249.
80. *Cal. Pat. 1391-96*, 591.
81. Hart, *Gloucester Cartulary* III, 236.
82. Graham Jones, 'The Market Place: form, location and antecedents' in Sylvia Pinches, Maggie Whalley and Dave Postles (eds.), *The Market Place and the Place of the Market* (Friends of the Centre for Local History, Leicester 9, 2004), 8.
83. John Rhodes, 'Review article' in *TBGAS,* 123 (2005), 188.
84. Archaeological Investigations Ltd., 'Castle House, Hereford', Internal archaeological reports 425 & 445 (1999) unpaginated.
85. Thorn, *Domesday: Hereford*, 6.10-11; 7.!, 5; 19.8; R. Fleming, 'Domesday Estates of the King and the Godwins' in *Speculum* 58 (1983), 1004-1006.
86. Sawyer, *Anglo-Saxon Charters*, 1101, 1102.
87. Ann Williams, 'Ralph 'called Ralph the Timid', earl of Hereford, magnate' in *Oxford DNB* (2004).
88. Stenton, *Anglo-Saxon England*, 569; Stanford, *Welsh Marches*, 204.
89. J.H. Round, *Feudal England* (1895), 320-6.
90. Douglas, *English Historical Documents*, 210-11.
91. Shoesmith, *Hereford Excavations* 2, 82-3.
92. John Williams (ed.), *Brut y Tywysogion* (Rolls Series, 1860), 42-3.
93. Lloyd, *History of Wales* II, 365; Thomas Jones (ed.), *Brenhineddy Saesson* (1971), 70-1.
94. Thomas Jones (ed.), *Brut y Tywysogyon – Peniarth* (1952), 14.
95. Ann Williams, 'The King's Nephew: The Family and Career of Ralph, Earl of Hereford' in Christopher Harper (ed.), *Studies in Medieval History presented to R. Allen Brown* (1989), 327-330.
96. Bruce Coplestone-Crow, 'The Fief of Alfred de Marlborough in Herefordshire in 1086' in *TWNFC* (1986), 377-5, 387-8.
97. Garmonsway, *Anglo-Saxon Chronicle*, 200.
98. *Ibid.*, 143-4, 181-2; Frank, Barlow, *Edward the Confessor* (1970), 124-5.
99. Williams, 'King's Nephew', 331 note 26.
100. Thorn, *Domesday: Hereford*, 6.10
101. C.P. Lewis, 'The Norman Settlement of Herefordshire under William I' in *Anglo-Norman Studies* 7 (1984), 196-7
102. Garmonsway, *Anglo-Saxon Chronicle*, 190.
103. Susan Reynolds, 'Eadric Silvaticus and the English Resistance' in *Bull. of Inst.of Hist. Research* 54 (1981), 102-3.
104. Ron Shoesmith, *A Guide to the Castles and Moated Sites of Herefordshire* (1996), 125.
105. Henry Hurst, 'The Archaeology of Gloucester Castle: An Introduction' in *TBGAS* 102 (1984), 73-128.
106. Hereford City Library (HCL), Pilley Collection 2326.
107. Hurst, 'Gloucester Castle', 80-1 – discusses other examples of Norman castles exploiting existing defences.
108. S.H. Martin, 'St Guthlac's Priory and the City Churches' in *TWNFC* (1954), 226.
109. Toby Purser, 'William fitz Osbern, Earl of Hereford: Personality and Power in the Welsh Frontier, 1066-71', in M. Strickland (ed.), *Armies, Chivalry and Warfare in Medieval Britain and France* (1998), 133-46.
110. R.C. Turner *et al.* 'The Great Tower, Chepstow Castle, Wales' in *The Antiquaries Jnl.* 84 (2004), 223-318. It is also suggested that fitzOsbern would not have needed a great hall at Chepstow as he took over one at Hereford! William I built the hall at Chepstow in *c.*1080 as a ceremonial centre for meeting the Welsh princes; Rick Turner & Andy Johnson (eds.), *Chepstow Castle* (2006), 21, 37-42, 60-61.

111. Thorn, *Herefordshire Domesday*, 2.1.
112. Lewis, 'Norman Settlement in Herefordshire', 203-4.
113. S.H. Martin, 'St. Guthlac's Priory', 219-27.
114. W.H. St John Hope, 'The Castle of Ludlow' in *Archaeologia* 61.1 (1908), 68.
115. Hart, *Gloucester Cartulary* I, 12, 85.
116. K.R. Potter (ed.), *Gesta Stephani* (1976), 108-11.
117. Stone & Appleton-Fox, *A View from Hereford's Past*, 108-11; Shoesmith, *Hereford City Excavations* 1, 39, 51, 129.
118. Hart, *Gloucester Cartulary* I, 85-6; *Regesta Regnum Anglo-Normanorum 1066-1154* II (1968), 139, 150, 308.
119. Christopher Brooke, 'St Peter of Gloucester and St Cadoc of Llancafan' in N. K. Chadwick (ed.), *Celtic and Saxon: Studies in the Early British Border* (1964), 259-272; Hart, *Gloucester Cartulary* I, 19, 93, 315; Dawn M. Hadley, 'The Historical Context of the Inhumation Cemetery at Bromfield, Shropshire' in *Trans. Salop Hist. and Arch. Soc.* (1995), 145-55.
120. Colvin, *King's Works* II, 676.
121. *Reg. Regnum* II, 150, 165; *Pipe Rolls (PR)* 1163, 7.
122. *PR* 1165, 110; 1173, 39; 1174, 121 – for brattices see D.J Cathcart King, *The Castle in England and Wales* (1988), 53-4; R. Higham & P. Barker, *Timber Castles* (1992), 362.
123. W. *Warren, Henry II* (1973), 129, 141; *PR* 1177, 52; 1178, 100; 1179, 39.
124. Colvin, *King's Works* II, 674; Higham & Barker, *Timber Castles*, 138-9.
125. David Whitehead, 'Historical background to the City Defences' in Shoesmith, *Hereford Excavations* 2, 18-21.
126. J.T. Appleby (ed.), *The Chronicle of Richard of Devizes* (1963), 30; *PR* 1190-91, 45; 1193-4, 86-7.
127. William Warren, *King John* (1961), 142-62.
128. *Ibid.*, 85-6; *PR* 1201, 264; 1202, 272-3.
129. *Turris* as a free standing stone tower is discussed in N.J.G. Pounds, *The Medieval Castle in England and Wales* (1990), 21-4; C Coulson, *Castles in Medieval Society*, (2003), *passim*; Higham and Barker, *Timber Castles*, 122, 132, 142 all suggest that a *turris* could also be constructed of timber
130. A.J. Taylor, *The King's Works in Wales* (1974), 306, 361.
131. Tom Mc Neill, *Castles in Ireland* (1997), 47, 57; H. Leask, *Irish Castles* (1951), 42-3; Joe Hillaby, 'Hereford Gold: Irish ,Welsh and English Land' in *TWNFC* (1988), 220.
132. *Ibid.*, 223-240.
133. Warren, *King John*, 103, 108, 121-2.
134. Thorn, *Herefordshire Domesday*, C.3.
135. S. Robinson, 'The Forests and Woodland Areas of Herefordshire' in *TWNFC* (1923), 203.
136. Warren, *King John*, 157; Hillaby, 'Hereford Gold', 242; Charles Young, *The Royal Forests of Medieval England* (1979), 25-6.
137. Martin, 'St Guthlac's Priory', 227; David Whitehead, 'Some Connected Thoughts on the Parks and Gardens of Herefordshire' in *TWNFC* (1995), 197-8.
138. J. Harvey, *Medieval Gardens* (1981), 80; *Inq. Misc. 1251-61*, 315; Charles & Emmanuel, *Cath. Muniments* III, 1178; *Pat. Rolls 1258-1266*, 431; A.T. Bannister, 'The Possessions of St Guthlac's Priory, Hereford' in *TWNFC* (1918), 38.
139. Harvey, *Medieval Gardens*, 86.
140. See note 29 in Whitehead, 'Some Connected Thoughts', 221.
141. Warren, *King John*, 217-19; Colvin, *King's Works* II, 119.
142. *Close Rolls 1237-42,* 254; *Liberate Rolls 1226-40*, 488; Colvin, *King's Works* II, 674-5.
143. See p. 45 below.
144. Chateau Gaillard probably cost Richard in the region of £7,000-£8,000 – R.A. Brown 'Royal Castle Building in England , 1154-1216' in Robert Liddiard (ed.), *Anglo-Norman Castles* (2003), 145. See also F.M. Powicke, *The Loss of Normandy* (1961), 190-6 and Coulson, *Castles in Medieval Society*, 147-8, which is less complimentary about its strength and stresses its symbolic role in Angevin diplomacy.
145. M. Gaimster & K. O'Coner (eds.), 'Medieval Britain and Ireland, 2005', *Medieval Archaeology,* 50. (2006), 322-3
146. *Liberate Rolls 1240-45*, 38, 260, 296; *Close Rolls 1237-42*, 254; *1242-3*, 443.
147. *Inq. Misc. 1392-1399*, 69; Lloyd, *History of Wales* II, 696.
148. *Close Rolls 1247-51*, 436; Shoesmith, *Castles and Moated Sites*, 128-9.
149. Pounds, *The Medieval Castle*, 109, 125; C.J. Robinson, *The Castles of Herefordshire* (1869), 75; J. Duncumb, *History and Antiquities* I, 234-5.
150. M. Powicke, *The Thirteenth Century* (1962), 189-97; Lloyd, *History of Wales* II, 734-5; *Cal. Misc. 1219-1307*, 100-101.
151. Lloyd, 736-8; Powicke, 197-203; Charles Hopkinson & Martin Speight, *The Mortimers: Lords of the March* (2002), 61-3.
152. *Cal. Pat. 1258-1266*, 478; *Liberate Rolls 1260-67*, 173, 175.
153. *Liberate Rolls 1267-72*, 88-9; *Close Rolls 1264-8*, 19, 59, 68; *Cal. Pat. 1258-66*, 610.
154. Duncumb, *History and Antiquities* I, 238-9.
155. Colvin, *King's Works* II, 675-6.
156. *Cal. Pat. 1324-7*, 337.
157. *Cal. Pat. 1343-49*, 418.
158. *Cal. Pat. 1281-92*, 514.

159. W.H. Cooke (ed.), *Duncumb's Collections towards the History and Antiquities of the County of Hereford* IV (1892), 96
160. Robinson, *Castles of Herefordshire*, 73; May Mc Kisack, *The Fourteenth Century* (1959), 465-7; Matthew Johnson, *Behind the Castle Gate* (2002), 139-42.
161. *Liberate Rolls 126-40*, 247; *Hist. MSS. Comm, 13th Report*, App. 4 (1892), 286; *Cal. Pat. 1391-96*, 213; *Lib. Rolls 1260-67*, 175.
162. *Cal. Pat. 1385-89*, 280.
163. *Cal. Pat. 1422-9*, 389; Hopkinson & Speight, *The Mortimers*, 127.
164. *Cal. Inq. Misc. 1392-99*, 69.
165. *Cal. Pat.1391-96*, 591.
166. Colvin, *King's Works*, 676.
167. B.G. Charles & H.D. Emmanuel, *Cathedral Muniments* II (1955), 1202.
168. *Cal. Fine Rolls 1471-55*, 74.
169. *Cath. Muns.* II, 1222; I, 1260.
170. Lucy Toulmin Smith, *The Itinerary of John Leland* II (1964), 64-5.
171. *Ibid.,* VI, 47.
172. *The Letters and Papers of Henry VIII 1509-13*, I, 896.
173. HRO, F.C. Morgan Transcripts of the Hereford City Records (sacks 1-7), f.31. Also, R. Johnson, *Ancient Customs of Hereford* (1882), 147.
174. *Cal. Pat. 1566-69*, 355; C.J. Robinson, *Mansions and Manors of Herefordshire* (1872), 43, 92, 104.
175. Mark Girouard, *Robert Smythson and the English Country House* (1983), 205-32 has a useful chapter discussing this issue.
176. HCL, Pilley Collection 2326 – contains original documents and transcripts, For North see *Old DNB* (Compact Edition) I, 1506.
177. *Ibid.,* – also repeated in Page's conveyance to Birch in August 1646.
178. John Webb, *Memorials of the Civil War in Herefordshire* I (1879), 160.
179. Duncumb *Collections* IV (1892), 96.
180. Webb, *Memorials* I, 277, 279.
181. *Ibid.,* II, 387.
182. *Ibid.,* I, 160-1.
183. Ian Atherton (ed.), *Sir Barnabus Scudamore's Defence against the Imputations of Treachery ... in 1645* (1992), 49.
184. HCL, Pilley 180, ff. 252-3.
185. John Webb (ed.), *The Military Memoir of Colonel John Birch* (Camden Society, 1873), 31.
186. Robinson (1872), 65; Webb I (1879), 160; *Cal. State Papers Domestic 1645-47* 21, 346; HCL, Pilley 2326.
187. HRO, LC Deeds 3929; E. Heath-Agnew, *Roundhead to Royalist* (1977), 48.
188. Webb I, 293-5; *Cal. State Papers Dom.* 21. 564.
189. HCL, Pilley 2326 & Thomas Bird, *Herefordiana* III (1827) – contains copies of original documents 'found amongst old papers at Eywood'; Heath-Agnew, 69-72.
190. HCL, Pilley 2326 – contains the entire correspondence with extracts from the Quarter Sessions Papers. See also Pilley Notebook 9, 2305.
191. Webb II, 301; *Cal. State Papers Dom. 1649-50* I, 119.
192. HCL, Civil War Pamphlets, *Imposter Magnus* (1654), 27-8 & *A Close Hypocrite Discovered* (1654), 18-19.
193. John Price, *An Historical Account of the City of Hereford* (1796), 51-4, 245-6.
194. *Hist. MSS. Comm. 13th Report* (1892), 346; HRO, Morgan Transcripts (sacks 16-19), f.292.
195. Webb II, 420-2; *Cal. State Papers Dom. 1655*, 136.
196. HRO, LC Deeds, 8458.
197. HCL, Pilley 2326 – here the events can be reconstructed from the Eywood papers and the extracts from the quarter sessions records made for Edward Harley. The volume is unfoliated.
198. HRO, F.C. Morgan transcripts (sacks 16-19), f.251; Charles Hadfield, *The Canals of South Wales and the Border* (1960), 185.
199. HCL, Pilley 2326 – has the original (?) pencil sketch, which is reproduced in *TWNFC*, XI (1884), opp.p. 162. Silvester appears in the Guildhall Library, London, Apprentice Register 1660 and Hereford Cathedral Library, Chapter Act Book 3, f.278v. and various references in the Fabric Accounts from 1684, but some of these are probably John Silvester jnr.
200. John Summerson in Howard Colvin (ed.), *Georgian London* (2003), 12-16.
201. HRO, Proceedings of the Common Council 1693-1707, f.26; John Eisel, 'The Castle Mills, Hereford' in *TWNFC* L (2000), 60-61.
202. HRO, Proceedings 1693-1707, ff. 43, 115; Minutes 1729-36, f.606; Quarter Sessions Order Book, Easter Session 1725; HCL, Topographical Catalogue, Old Corporation Deeds.
203. HRO, Hereford City MSS. V, f.113.
204. HRO, HLM/A2 Minutes 1708-54 (mutilated volume), f.457; Quarter Sessions Order Book, 15 July 1712; HCL, Pilley 2326.
205. HCL, Pilley 2326 – Eywood letters.
206. C.H. & M. Collins Baker, *The Life and Circumstances of James Brydges, First Duke of Chandos* (1949), 27.
207. *Ibid.*, 213; Andor Gomme, *Smith of Warwick* (2000), 231-2.
208. HRO, C99/III/140.

209. HRO, A81/IV/386.

210. HCL, Pilley 2326; Collins Baker, *Life and Circumstances*, 265-74.

211. HCL, Pilley 2326 – Eywood letter.

212. HCL, Bird III, f.247 – quoting Quarter Sessions, 15 July 1735; David Whitehead, *The Country Houses of Herefordshire* (forthcoming); Peter Martin, *Pursuing Innocent Pleasures: The Gardening World of Alexander Pope* (1984), 22, 31.

213. Hereford Cathedral Archives (HCA), Catalogue of Post-Medieval Documents, 3389; Robinson, *Mansions* (1872), 39.

214. Christopher Morris (ed.), *The Journeys of Celia Fiennes* (1959), 44; Joseph Jones, *Hereford Cathedral and City* (1858), 87.

215. HRO, Quarter Session Order Book, 3 October 1752; Jones, *Hereford*, 85.

216. HRO, Quarter Sessions, 8 April 1755, 15 January 1760.

217. William Rees, *Hereford Guide* (1827), 93. A similar 'dining club' with pantheistic interests appears to have flourished around Painswick in Gloucestershire, in the mid-18th century – Tim Mowl, 'In the Realm of the Great God Pan' in *Country Life*, 17 October 1996, 54-59.

218. The minute book of the society from 1786-1831 is in the Hereford City Library manuscript collection, No. 367. What follows, unless otherwise indicated, is derived from this source.

219. Charles Renton, *The Story of Herefordshire's Hospitals* (1999), 27-8.

220. Duncumb's career is assessed by Philip Riden in John Duncumb, *Collections towards ... County of Hereford* I, part I (Merton Press edition, 1966), vi-xix.

221. Stephen Daniels, Susanne Seymour and Charles Watkins, 'Border Country: The Politics of the Picturesque in the Middle Wye Valley' in Michael Rosenthal, Christiana Payne, and Scott Wilcox (eds.), *Prospects for the Nation: Recent Essays in British Landscape 1750-1880*, Yale Studies in British Art 4 (1998), 157-63.

222. Owen Jones (ed.), *The Myvyrian Archaiology of Wales* (1870), passim; on the traditions of the lost province of Wales 'between the Wye and the Severn' see John Lloyd, *A History of Wales* I (1939), chapter 8.

223. *HJ*, 4 May 1775.

224. *HJ* 29 January 1784.

225. Worcester Record Office, BA 10470/2/294, f.13v.

226. Rees, *Hereford Guide*, 84.

227. *HJ*, 11 March 1779.

228. HRO, Q/CM/2 Memorandum Book 1.

229. *HJ* 7 November 1782. Thomas Symonds is to be found in Howard Colvin, *A Biographical Dictionary of British Architects 1600-1840* (1995), 945-6.

230. HRO, Quarter Sessions Records, 13 January 1784; HCL, Temper Minutes, 11 April 1804; Sarah M. Couch, 'The Practice of Avenue Planting in the Seventeenth and Eighteenth Centuries', *Garden History* 20 (1992), 181-2; *TWNFC* (1868), 88.

231. HRO, Q/CM/2.

232. *HJ* 30 September 1779; 20 March 1777.

233. HRO, GHI/160-171.

234. Illustrated in David Whitehead & Ron Shoesmith, *James Wathen's Herefordshire 1770 –1820* (1994), Pl. 17; Rees, *Hereford Guide*, note on p. 86.

235. C. Bruyn Andreas (ed.), *The Torrington Diaries* I (1934), 127, 315. Price, *Historical Account* (1796), 72 describes the Infirmary as 'an elegant modern building ... [in a] pleasant healthy situation ... on the banks of the River Wye ... highly eligible for the purpose'.

236. *HJ* 10 November 1785; 17 November 1785, 11 August 1802.

237. HRO, Quarter Sessions Records, 12 July 1768.

238. HCA, 4491.

239. HRO, Quarter Sessions Records, 10 July 1787, 2 October 1787.

240. A copy of Simon Fisher's watercolour is in HCL, Pilley 2327; Rees, *Hereford Guide*, 85; William Collins, *Modern Hereford* II (1911), 12.

241. *Ibid.*, 7; David Morris, *Thomas Hearne and his Landscape* (1989), Pls. 36, 87.

242. *HJ* 27 May 1793, 12 September 1798; Rees, *Hereford Guide*, 256.

243. Hereford Art Gallery and illustrated in Jim & Muriel Tonkin, *The Book of Hereford* (1975), 39.

244. *HJ* 17 November 1785, 4 November 1789; Symonds – HRO, A 95/V/EL/285.

245. Whitehead & Shoesmith, *Wathen*, Pl. 18.

246. Mavis Batey & David Lambert, *The English Garden Tour* (1990), 183; *HJ* 19 December 1770.

247. Rees, *Hereford Guide*, 24.

248. Malcolm Andrews, *The Search for the Picturesque* (1989), 41-50.

249. Sidney & Beatrice Webb, *English Poor Law History* I (1927), 83-5.

250. HCL, Pilley, 2326.

251. HRO, Quarter Sessions, 11 July 1705, 7 October 1729.

252. R. Shoesmith and R. Crosskey, 'Go to Gaol…in Hereford' in *TWNFC* XLVIII (1994), 110-11.

253. HRO, Quarter Sessions, 9 October 1735, 13 July 1742, 14 July 1747, 16 July 1754, 13 July 1762.

254. *Ibid.*, 15 July 1777, 18 April 1778, 12 January 1779.

255. *HJ* 28 July 1785.
256. Shoesmith and Crosskey, *TWNFC* (1994), 109.
257. Colvin, *Dictionary,* 945-6; HRO, AE13/1; HCL, Herefordshire Scraps. II, 53v; HRO, Downton T74/413.
258. HRO, Quarter Sessions, 6 October 1789, 27 January 1790. The story of John Nash and the new gaol is told by David Whitehead, 'John Nash and Humphry Repton' in *TWNFC* XLVII (1992), 211-213.
259. HRO, Quarter Session, 12 July 1796; *HJ* 12 October 1796.
260. HCL, Pilley 2326 – letters at the back of the scrapbook; *HJ* 10 September 1800.
261. Charles & Emanuel, *Cath. Muns.* 338, 987.
262. David Whitehead, 'In Search of St Ethelbert's Well' in *HAN* 35 (1978), 11.
263. HRO, Council Minutes 1755-78, f.160; Improvement Commissioners Minute Book 1778-1810, ff. 44, 88.
264. HRO, Guildhall Collection GH1/172-80.
265. John Allen, *Hereford Guide* (1806), 67.
266. John Pyndar Wright, *A Walk through Hereford* (1819), 44-6; Ella Mary Leather, *Folk-Lore of Herefordshire* (1912), 12-14.
267. Ex. Inf. The late Dr. & Mrs. Paulo of Well Cottage, Quay Street.
268. Rees, *Hereford Guide*. 67.
269. *Ibid.,* 68; Jones, *Cathedral and City,* 85; *Hereford Times* (*HT*), 28 September 1872 - also in HCL, Pilley 2281, f. 78.
270. Alfred Watkins, 'The King's Ditch of the City of Hereford' in *TWNFC* XXIII (1926), 155; Whitehead *HAN* 35, 12.
271. *Hereford Civic Trust Newsletter* 14 (1977), 11.
272. *HJ* 4 August 1802.
273. Edward Gill, *Nelson and the Hamilton's on Tour* (1987), 61-2.
274. *Ibid.*, 65-6; *HJ* 23 August 1802.
275. *HJ* 13 November 1805; Gill, *Nelson*, 56.
276. *HJ* 13 November 1805, 20 November 1805.
277. *HJ* 4 December 1805, 11 December 1805, 18 December 1805, 8 January 1806.
278. Colvin, *Dictionary,* 458-60.
279. HCA, 5695 Survey and Plan 1786; *HJ* 28 September 1786, 26 April 1787.
280. HRO, Q/AS/1-3; HCL, Pilley Scrapbook I, f.80.
281. *HJ* I Januray 1806.
282. *HJ* 2 April 1806, 9 April 1806. Wood takes over Symonds' yard –*HJ* 17 August 1802.
283. *HJ* 16 August 1809, 18 March 1812. Thomas Late – HRO, Hereford Improvement Commission Minutes, ff. 272, 310, 346; Gaol Work Q/FV/6.
284. *Winkles' History and Descriptive Account of the Cathedral Church of Hereford* (W.H. Vale, publisher, Hereford, 1842), Pl. 3.
285. Rees, *Hereford Guide*, 68; Jones, *Cathedral and City* (1858), 87; HCL, Pilley, Herefordshire Scraps II, f.56.
286. *HT* 9 December 1875, 16 December 1875.
287. Roy Porter, 'Material Pleasures in the Consumer Society' in Roy Porter & Marie Mulvey Roberts (eds.), *Pleasure in the Eighteenth Century* (1996), 22-4, 27-8.
288. Paul Elliott, 'The Derby Arboretum: the first specially designed Municipal Public Park in Britain' in *Midland History* XXVI (2001), 147-55.
289. Price, *Historical Account*, 74. For Price's background see Norman Reeves, 'Five Leominster Historians' in *TWNFC* XLV (1985), 287-9.
290. HCL, MSS. 367, Tempers Minute Book, *passim*.
291. Richard Warner, *Literary Recollections* I (1830), 388.
292. HCL, Tempers Minutes, 5 November 1818.
293. *Ibid.*, 18 March 1819. For Charles Heather see Colvin, *Dictionary*, 486 and *HJ* 10 June 1812.
294. HCL, Tempers Minutes, 4 November 1831; Rees, *Hereford Guide*, 84.
295. HCL, LC, 367, Hereford Castle Green Reading Room and Baths Minute Book 1830-59 – unfoliated. Unless otherwise indicated, the following section is based upon this source.
296. Colvin, *Architects*, 880; *HJ* 28 July 1824.
297. *HJ* 5 August 1824, 25 August 1824.
298. HCL, Baths Minute Book, passim; William Collins, *Modern Hereford* II (1911), 110-11.
299. HCL, Baths Minute Book, 23 September 1856, 12 January 1857.
300. Jones, *Cathedral and City,* 14-15; *HT* 10 March 1875, 24 March 1875. Also in HCL, Pilley 2281, f.51.
301. *Ibid.*
302. J.H. Ross, 'Founder of the Woolhope Club' and Jean O' Donnell, 'The Hereford Free Library 1871-1912' in David Whitehead & John Eisel (eds.), *A Herefordshire Miscellany* (2000), 18-25, 124-37.
303. *HJ* 28 July 1824; Eisel, *TWNFC* (2000), 64.
304. T.W. Rammel, *Report to the General Board of Health into the Sewage of the City of Hereford* (1853), 35, 44 and T. Curley, *Hereford Sanitary Improvements Report* (1854); Eisel, *TWNFC* (2000), 65-6; Ron Shoesmith, *The Castle Pool: An Historical and Archaeological Assessment* (1999), 7-8.
305. HCL, Baths Minute Book, 13 January 1832.

306. Eisel, *TWNFC* (2000), 66.
307. Collins, *Modern Hereford*, 110-1.
308. Edward Brayley & John Britton, *The Beauties of England and Wales* VI (1805), 490.
309. Uvedale Price, *Essays on the Picturesque* I (1810), 57.
310. Jones, *Cathedral and City*, 86.
311. Collins, *Modern Hereford*, 112; John Murray, *Handbook for Travellers in Worcestershire and Herefordshire* (1894), 98.
312. Ron Shoesmith, *Alfred Watkins* (1990), 142-4; David Whitehead, *Yesterday's Town: Hereford* (1983), 66.
313. Whitehead & Eisel, *Miscellany* (2000), 146-7.
314. Jones, *Cathedral and City*, 88.
315. HRO, BG11/9/Fg – Castle Green Minutes 1872-6.
316. The following section is based upon HRO, BG11/9/Db/1-2 – four volumes of the City Council's Estates Committee1871-1914. The major events in the improvement of the Green are also summarised in William Collins, *Modern Hereford*. I (1911), 110-13.
317. Alfred Watkins, 'Foundations of Buildings in Herefoord Castle', *TWNFC* (1933) 39.
318. *HJ* 20 March 1777
319. Collins, *Modern Hereford*, 112. For the debate about the sheep – *HJ* 6 April 1901.
320. Renton, *Herefordshire's Hospitals*, 38.
321. Watkins, *TWNFC* (1933), 38
322. *HJ* 8 July 1893.
323. Watkins, *TWNFC* (1933), 38; *HJ* 19 June 1897, 26 June 1897; Whitehead, *Yesterday's Town,* 96, 106-7; Anne Sandford, *Hereford in Old Photographs* (1987), 71, 94.
324. This section, unless otherwise stated, is based upon postcards and photographs in the possession of the author, Derek Foxton, Hereford Record Office and Hereford City Library.
325. Hazel Conway, *People's Parks: the design and development of Victorian parks in Britain* (1991), *passim*.
326. *HT* 8 July 1893, *HJ* 6 April 1901.
327. William Collins, *Historical Landmarks of Hereford* (1915), 114-5; Watkins, *TWNFC* (1933), 38.
328. Most of the material in this section, unless otherwise indicated, is based upon (1) the pre- Second World War Council Minutes deposited in the Hereford Reference Library and (2) Hereford City Records Addendum AW 46 in the Hereford Record Office. These collections have only been sampled in this study. Footnotes have been used for the most significant developments.
328. HCL, City Council Minutes, Estates Committee, 26 April 1932.
330. David Whitehead, *A Survey of the Historic Parks and Gardens of Herefordshire* (2001), 352.
331. HCL, Council Minutes, 10 May 1934, 14 June 1934.
332. HRO, AW46/Box56/1100.
333. Graham Roberts, *The Shaping of Modern Hereford* (2001), 192.
334. HCL, *Hereford Civic Trust Newsletters* 1-3 (1973).

Index